The Fortifications of
ALDERNEY

Colin Partridge & Trevor Davenport

**Published on behalf of
The Alderney Fortifications Centre
by
Alderney Publishers, Alderney, Channel Islands**

First published in Great Britain in 1993 by
Alderney Publishers,
Alderney,
Channel Islands.

British Library Cataloguing in Publication Data
Partridge, Colin
    Fortifications of Alderney:
    Concise History and Guide to the Defences of
    Alderney from Roman Times to the
    Second World War
    I. Title II. Davenport, Trevor George
    914.234304

ISBN 0-9517156-0-7

Designed by Colin Partridge

Printed and bound in Guernsey by
GP Printers,
P.O. Box 57,
Braye Road, Vale,
Guernsey, C.I.

CONTENTS

PREFACE

This work has taken longer to reach publication than the authors would have wished; it has been even longer (almost three decades) in gestation. If nothing else, it should have benefited from affording the authors the luxury of extending their research and demolishing some of the many received myths which have arisen over the years in their subject; this is part of a continuing process.

It is entirely appropriate that the publication of this work should have been undertaken by the Alderney Fortifications Centre which was formed in 1978 in the aftermath of the deliberate destruction carried out with official sanction at Fort Albert the previous year. Composed of just three people, all of whom are members of the Fortress Study Group (FSG), the Alderney Fortifications Centre has lobbied privately and publicly, when the need has arisen, for the recognition of the island's military architecture of all periods as buildings worthy of protection. In 1981, they were successful in making Alderney the location for the annual conference of the FSG, since when much wider concern for the future of these outstanding works has been expressed.

In the preparation of this publication, the authors wish to acknowledge, with gratitude, the debt which they owe to Major C. A. Hynes and his wife, Elizabeth, not only for their hospitality and unstinting encouragement, but for having been instrumental in the formation of the Alderney Fortifications Centre.

Colin Partridge/Trevor Davenport   Alderney: September, 1993

Acknowledgements
The authors wish to acknowledge the kind permission received to reproduce photographs in this book from the copyright holders whose names appear in the captions. Unless otherwise stated, all photographs are by Colin Partridge.

Cover
An aerial view of Alderney harbour and Braye Bay from the north-west with Fort Grosnez in the foreground.

INTRODUCTION

The Channel Islands have been part of the Duchy of Normandy since 933 A.D. and although the mainland of Normandy was lost to England in the thirteenth century, they have remained loyal to the Crown ever since despite their proximity to and periodic attacks from France.

Alderney, the most northerly of the Channel Islands, is approximately 3.5 miles (5.5km) long and 1.5 miles (2.4km) broad. It is the nearest of the larger islands to France, being approximately 8 miles (13km) west of Cap de la Hague at the northern tip of the Cotentin Peninusula and 25 miles (40km) from Cherbourg. Guernsey is 24 miles (39km) to the south-west; Jersey is 30 miles (48km) and the coast of Brittany is 70 miles (113km) due south; to the north Portland is 60 miles (97km) distant.

The island is higher in the west with a maximum elevation of over 290 feet (88m), while the eastern end is low-lying with numerous small bays. The high ground is generally plateau-like with steep cliffs on the western and southern flanks.

To the north, between Alderney and the small island of Burhou, is a navigable channel known as The Swinge, while to the east The Race separates the island from the Cotentin Peninsula. There are formidable tide rips and overfalls in both channels which, together with the treacherous rocks and reefs surrounding the island, have acted as important natural defences throughout the island's history.

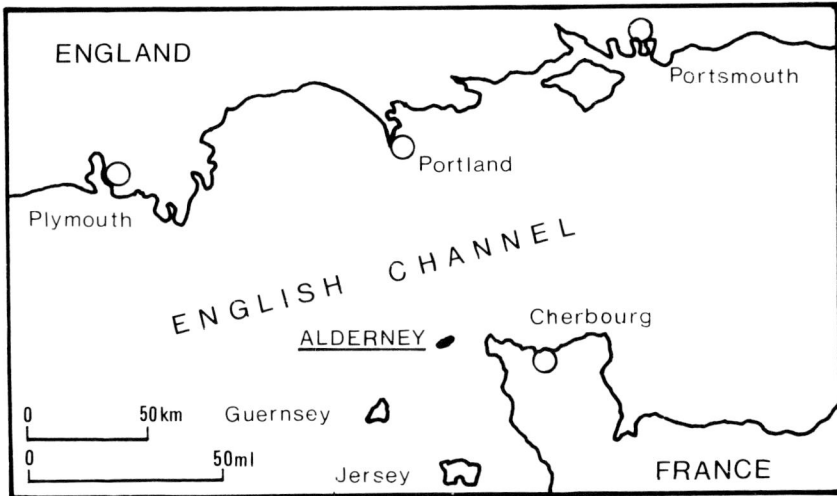

1. FROM EARLIEST TIMES

The strategic value of Alderney

The megalithic cist, which lies off the road above Fort Tourgis, is the oldest known surviving man-made structure in Alderney. This prehistoric burial chamber, known as Roc à L'Épine, was built about 4,000 years ago and undoubtedly is one of many such tombs that have been destroyed during the subsequent periods of fortification. It is reported that many of the uprights and capstones were used in the Victorian forts and breakwater, while a few remained only to be destroyed during the construction of some German works. Fortunately, many of the prehistoric sites were recorded by the Lukis family of Guernsey between 1838 and 1853, otherwise their locations would now be lost to historians.

In 1832, a hoard of more than two hundred late Bronze Age implements, dating from about 800 BC, was found buried on Longis Common, while in 1853 two bronze halberd heads of an earlier period were discovered during the building of Château à L'Étoc. A more recent discovery was made in 1968 at Les Huguettes where a quantity of early Iron Age pottery was found during an archaeological excavation.

Two of these discoveries were made close to Longis Bay, the island's only sheltered anchorage at the time. It was natural that settlement should occur in this area, just as it was natural that the Romans should have built defences there too. Roman artefacts have been discovered in the Longis Common area, both at the Kennels and the small fort known today as the Nunnery which is probably built on late Roman foundations. The origins of the Nunnery are still the subject of debate, although its outline and foundations are certainly Roman in character. Johnston (1981) points out that the use of Roman material in the fabric and herring-bone masonry are not indicators of Roman date, but that the substantial offset just below ground level is a Roman technique. If the plan is compared with the five signal-stations of the Yorkshire coast, then the gently rounded corners, the original single entrance (on the south face) and the small functionally insignificant half-round towers certainly support a Roman date. Although Johnston postulates that the Alderney site served a double role of signal station and naval base, he points out that Essex Hill would have been a better location being visible both from the other islands and the French mainland.

Ewen, in his article *Alderney and the Saxon Shore*, proposed that the Romans first established a base at Longis to assist in the protection of shipments of food supplies from Britain to the continent. The

The Nunnery (above) still exhibits the rudimentary round towers. The plan (below) shows the former barracks (A) now converted into two dwellings, a German personnel shelter (B), the site of the Napoleonic magazine (C), the collapsed outer section of wall (D) and the later entrance (E) (after Johnson).

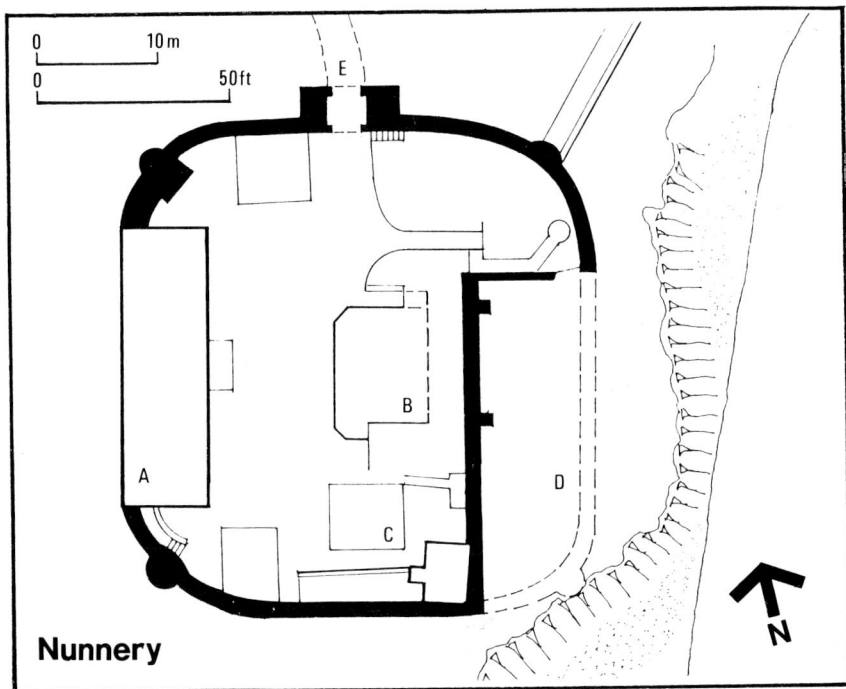

island was ideally placed to act as an advanced outpost from which to watch for and launch an attack against enemy shipping. He bases his suggestions on a study of the *Notitia Dignitatum,* a comparative register of all the civil and military establishments in the Roman Empire about 400 A.D.

For nearly five hundred years after the departure of the Romans, Europe and the Channel Islands were subjected to sudden raids by Norsemen. In 933 AD, Rollo, a chieftain of Viking descent who had assumed the title of Duke of Normandy after capturing large tracts of land from the West Franks, added the islands to his duchy.

The first documented reference to Alderney occurs in a charter of 1042, when Duke William (the Conqueror) granted Alderney to the monastery of Mont St. Michel by way of compensation for loss of property in Guernsey. Fifteen years later it had passed to Geoffrey de Mowbray, Bishop of Coutances. By 1263 the diocese still retained half the island with the other half belonging to William L'Ingenieur, Lord of Alderney; subsequently William's sons sold it back to the Crown. By now France had become an enemy and successive bishops had great difficulty in maintaining their authority.

In 1204, King John lost most of his French possessions and the Channel Islands became of much greater importance to the English Crown. The subsequent building of strong fortifications in Jersey and Guernsey reflected their new strategic value, but Alderney was left undefended.

At the beginning of the Hundred Years War in 1338, Alderney was attacked and looted by the French. For the next 150 years, records for the island are very sparse, but it is apparent that during the fifteenth century the small township around the Trigale and St. Martins expanded eastwards from the Marais to include Le Bourgage and housed a population of some seven hundred. Longis Bay was still the only safe anchorage and on the west side, at low-water, the remains of the old stone jetty may still be seen.

Towards the end of the fifteenth century, Pope Sixtus IV issued a papal bull of neutrality recognising the Channel Islands as neutral territory during any conflict between England and France. This neutrality was maintained until after the accession of Henry VIII, even though war again broke out between the two countries. However, towards the end of Henry's reign, with the increase in sea-borne trade and the activities of pirates, the French made plans to take the uninhabited island of Sark as the Islands had now assumed a considerable strategic value. Consequently, the English authorities, realising the value of Alderney as both a naval base and a haven from privateers, authorised the construction of a powerful fort which would dominate the approaches to the harbour at Longis.

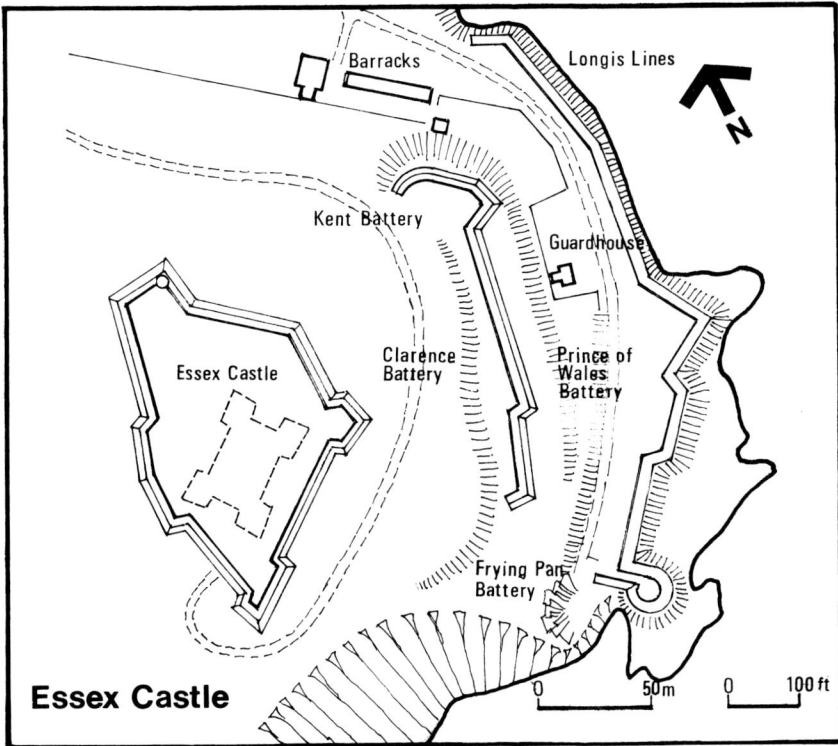

This notional trace of Essex Castle, based on plans surviving from the early 1800s, also locates the adjoining early coastal batteries.

Construction began in 1546 during the last year of Henry's reign and was continued after his death by the Protector Somerset. A labour force of over 200 men and a garrison of 200 soldiers were sent to Alderney under the command of Captain Robert Turberville and the French seizure of Sark in 1549 ensured that work continued. After Somerset's fall from power later in the year, all construction came to a halt only to be resumed at intervals over the next four years. A report submitted by Captain Richard Broke, who had been ordered to survey the situation in Alderney, recommended that work be continued and in July 1550, £1000 was voted for further work on the fort. However, by November the garrison was permanently reduced to 100 men. In 1552, Thomas Barnabe, a government agent, urged in a letter to a member of the Privy Council that greater importance should be attached to Alderney because of its strategic value for the interception of French shipping.

The north and west walls of Essex Castle are the only remnants of the original sixteenth century work.

On the death of Edward VI and the accession of the catholic Mary in 1553, it was finally decided to abandon the project in 1554 on the grounds that it was expensive and of no benefit to the realm. Thus ended the first half-hearted attempt by the government to fortify the island.

Only the north and west walls of this original structure remain now incorporated into the later Victorian work known as Essex Barracks and Hospital. The very few available records describe the fort's outer walls as being a refuge for islanders and their animals which suggests that these walls may be of an earlier date still. This would seem to be confirmed by the absence of any ramparts, embrasures or firing steps on the north and west walls. Engineers John Ridgeway and John Rogers, who had been employed in the defences of Boulogne, where they had come under the influence of Italian engineers, were sent to Alderney to advise on the new works. No contemporary plans appear to have survived, but a later map of the island indicates a regular, square plan enclosing a small area with four rounded bastions. The records of the Privy Council show that a programme of construction was sustained for several years and that the work was supplied with ordnance at a cost of over £5,000. However, it should be noted that where representations of a defensive work appear on later maps of the island, they vary in form and cannot be relied upon for accuracy of trace.

The name 'Essex' given to this and the subsequent Victorian work, dates from the Le Mesurier family in the eighteenth century when they popularised the idea that the Earl of Essex built the fort; records show that construction was abandoned before the Earl was born. The name Essex Castle is not found before 1770, and until then it is referred to as the Upper Fort or Les Murs de Haut. In the list of properties discharged by John Le Mesurier when he surrendered the lease of the island in 1825, the site is referred to as Fort Hill.

In 1558, four years after the fort had been abandoned and the garrison withdrawn, Alderney was looted by a Captain Malesart, a French soldier of fortune. His decision to return for more booty was an unfortunate one as his expedition was captured by a force dispatched by the Governor of Guernsey and Malesart was incarcerated in the Tower of London. The Governor of Guernsey at this time was Sir Leonard Chamberlain and this incident began a long relationship between Alderney and the Chamberlain family.

The looting of Alderney was followed later in the year by the death of Mary, the accession of Elizabeth I and, in the following year, a peace treaty was once again signed with France. In 1560, Sir Leonard brought the Privy Council's attention to the weak state of Alderney's defences. He pointed out that the island and its inhabitants had no ordnance "to withstand the simplest rover that approaches them", but the plea appeared to have produced no results. Although the island was in no state to defend itself, in 1564 forty pirates, who were operating from Alderney, were arrested and taken to Guernsey.

By 1566 Francis Chamberlain, who had succeeded his father Sir Leonard as Governor of Guernsey, once again raised the question of Alderney's defences with the Privy Council. He stressed that the 800 inhabitants should be retained to provide comfort for travellers, to fish for conger and mackerel, and to annoy the enemy and assist in invasion. More importantly he believed that the island would be a scourge in enemy hands and considerably increase the costs of defending the other islands. Should it be decided to abandon Alderney then "It should be considered whether any petty forts and blockhouses in the realm should be spared . . . the Fort begun and Longie's tower should be blown up and the harbours choked to prevent the enemy using them." The reference to "the Fort begun" is obviously to the unfinished Upper Fort, while "Longie's tower" is probably part of the Lower Fort (the Nunnery), although when it was built is unknown. Whether any action was taken by the Council is not recorded, but it is plain that the Chamberlains were in favour of defending Alderney as George was lessee of the island.

After the Council had received a request in 1575 from the islanders for protection against French raids, some ordnance seems to have been sent as three years later four brass cannon were replaced by iron pieces. The reason given was that the guns were liable to be taken by raiders and that brass guns were too valuable to lose!

After receiving his patent in 1584, John Chamberlain, George's brother, took up residence in the Nunnery. The patent was granted on condition that "he should drive out our enemies, pirates and robbers from Alderney" and that he should keep forty male English residents on the island. It was not long before he upset the inhabitants and the Privy Council became alarmed by the state of unrest in the island which possessed such strategic importance in the imminent conflict with Spain. The Council drew up a set of ordinances which defined the respective rights of John Chamberlain and the islanders which it was hoped would keep the people contented and also ensure that the island would be strengthened and defended against potential enemies. However, in 1588, the Armada bypassed the Islands and Alderney's new defences remained untested.

John Chamberlain was forced to sell his rights in Alderney to the Earl of Essex in 1591, who in turn granted a lease back to John's son William. In 1608 William Chamberlain submitted a report to the Privy Council which described the island and made proposals for its development. He states that the island is not guardable and that John Chamberlain had made a dwelling in "an old castle of small strength" and had assisted the inhabitants to defend themselves; he notes that prior to this, the island had been "a refuge for pirates and such lewd persons (and) that there is in the Island a decayed fort which being repaired would give sufficient strength to the Inhabitants to retire into in tyme of danger and to withstand any suddaine attempt of the enemye." The "castle of small strength" obviously refers to the Nunnery, while the "decayed fort" refers to the castle left unfinished by Turberville. This implies that no repairs had been carried out to this fort and that it was not habitable.

The question of the inadequacy of Alderney's defences again became of importance in 1627 after the failure of Buckingham's expedition at La Rochelle provoked the threat of a French retaliatory assault on the Channel Islands. In April 1628, munitions and ordnance were dispatched without delay for the protection of Alderney, but this scare soon passed as the Governor of Guernsey destroyed the French fleet.

After the outbreak of the English Civil War in 1642, both Guernsey and Alderney were held by parliamentary forces and in 1643 an officer was sent to Alderney from Guernsey with the express purpose of putting the island in a state of defence against the royalist forces holding Jersey. It is possible that some form of island Militia had existed for centuries, but it is not until 1657, when Captain Nicholas Ling was transferred to Alderney from Sark as Governor, that a Commander of the Militia is officially recorded. In 1679, Ling died at the age of 80 while still retaining the command of the Militia. Five years later the governorship passed to Thomas Le Mesurier, and the island and command of the Militia was effectively to remain in the hands of the Le Mesurier family for the next hundred years.

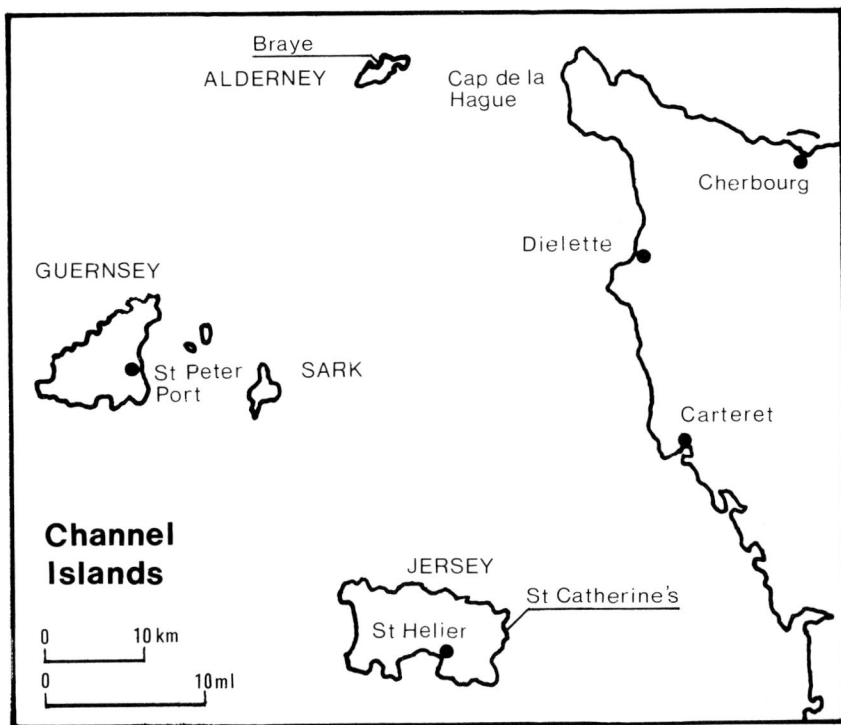

Braye
ALDERNEY
Cap de la Hague
Cherbourg
Dielette
GUERNSEY
St Peter Port
SARK
Carteret
Channel Islands
JERSEY
St Catherine's
St Helier
0 10 km
0 10 ml

In 1736, to stimulate trade, Henry Le Mesurier was granted part of the common lands at Braye to build houses and warehouses on condition that he constructed a jetty there to replace the one at Longis. A few years later, the Board of Ordnance called for a survey of Alderney for the purpose of siting new batteries. The survey was completed in 1739 by Colonel J. H. Bastide and his map shows the jetty as the "New Peer" which still exists today known as the Douglas Quay. Bastide's map lists the sites for ten proposed batteries mounting 27 guns in all, a considerable improvement on previous attempts to fortify the island.

With the outbreak of the Seven Years War in 1756, the new harbour at Braye became a base for privateers; the ships were fitted out by the Le Mesuriers and crewed by islanders who took to their newly-acquired occupation with great resolve and Alderney prospered. By 1770 the Militia consisted of 200 men who were armed by the British Government. Every man between 16 and 60 was obliged "to Carry Arms and do Duty whenever the Governor deems it necessary to require his Services."

Relations with France remained tense and concern was expressed that an alliance with the emerging states of America during the War of Independence would place additional strain on Britain's maritime defence. These fears were realised in 1779 when a French naval force attacked Elizabeth Castle in Jersey and, three years later, when troops were landed on that island's west coast and only defeated by the 95th Regiment of Foot commanded by Major Francis Peirson, who was fatally wounded in the battle for St. Helier.

In 1777 Colonel Peter Le Mesurier, the eldest son of John who had taken over the governorship from his brother Henry, reorganised the Alderney Militia and turned it into an efficient unit. Four years later, uniforms were adopted for the first time. John died in 1793 and Peter Le Mesurier became governor at the outbreak of the French Revolutionary Wars. Three hundred men were immediately sent by the government to assist in the defence of Alderney, where the Royal Artillery had already established a company of invalid gunners to form the core of the coastal artillery. The senior officer of the garrison force was appointed Fort Major, and this was to lead to serious differences of opinion with the Governor over the command of the troops in the island in the years ahead.

For more than twenty years, the military superiority of France on the European continent placed great pressures on the Channel Islands and led to three successive periods of potential assault. Detailed plans laying down the precise forces and measures for launching an expedition against the Islands as early as February 1794 were contained in a decree of the National Convention. Again, in 1797 and 1801, forces were being assembled in the Channel ports in preparation for an invasion of the English south coast. During this period of greatest threat, the Islands played a valuable role as stations for shipping charged with the surveillance and blockade of the French ports, and providing regular intelligence to the Admiralty. Small vessels stationed at Alderney acted as scouts under the command of Phillippe d'Auvergne in Jersey.

The survey carried out by Bastide in 1739 had recommended that ten batteries mounting 27 guns should be constructed, but few of these recommendations were implemented. However, in 1795 when the frigate *Amethyst* was wrecked on the coast, the guns were got up, carriages and ammunition were supplied by the Board of Ordnance and batteries were constructed at the state's expense. In succeeding years the garrison was strengthened with additional numbers of invalid gunners and soldiers. In 1803, when hostilities with France were renewed after the false Peace of Amiens, the garrison and defences were placed under Major-General Sir John Doyle then commanding the forces in Guernsey.

Major-General (later Lieutenant-General) Sir John Doyle, GCB, KC who served as Lieutenant-Governor of Guernsey from 1803-1816, worked tirelessly for the improvement of the Bailiwick's defences during the Napoleonic Wars (Government House, Guernsey).

Once again, preparations for imminent invasion by the French led to a call for speedy reinforcement of troops within the Bailiwick by Sir John Doyle and Alderney was placed in an immediate state of defence. At the Lieutenant-Governor's insistence a series of military surveys of Alderney were carried out with a view to improving the numbers and strength of the coastal artillery. The attention of the government was repeatedly called to the defenceless state of the island and the "perplexity and alarm" in which the inhabitants were kept, believing that they no longer enjoyed their sovereign's protection. Armed cutters stationed at Alderney continued to provide the Admiralty with shipping intelligence, and in 1809 the Lieutenant-Governor approved recommendations for telegraphic communication between the Island with the proposal to erect a tower on Beacon Heights, employing Mr Mulgrave's semaphore system.

By this date, thanks to the efforts principally of Sir John Doyle, Alderney's coastal defences mounted some 93 pieces of ordnance in nineteen batteries, with barrack accommodation for a total force of 568 men. Writing to his sisters in August 1806, Brigadier-General J. Mackenzie in command of the troops in Alderney lamented; "From this sterile place I can give you nothing entertaining — there is but little society, but the place is healthy." His detailed orders for signalling the approach of hostile shipping, the mustering of forces and the manning of batteries are a graphic description of conditions in Alderney at this time of great tension. The Alderney Militia, comprising artillerymen, grenadiers and light infantry totalling some 384 men, provided a valuable contribution to the island's protection, and would shortly be issued with new muskets by the government, while approval had even been granted for the augmentation of a small cavalry unit.

Notwithstanding these improvements, Sir John Doyle sustained his attack on the government to remove the deficiencies which he still saw in Alderney's defences, and this was renewed in 1810 when another threat of assault by the French was perceived. The loss of Alderney would, he claimed, seriously threaten the security of Guernsey and Jersey, and he offered to defray part of the cost from his own pocket of implementing recommendations put forward the previous year by a distinguished group of officers. These included the construction of two Sussex towers on the Houmet de Longis (Raz Island) and at Mannez, a place of arms at Touraille (the present site of Fort Albert) and various improvements in the existing lines and batteries. In spite of the outbreak of war with the United States in 1812, these works were never implemented and with the collapse of Napoleon's empire in 1814 and his final defeat at Waterloo in 1815, their whole *raison d'être* was removed.

By 1815 not only had the French Revolutionary and Napoleonic struggles ended, but a century and a quarter of almost continuous war with France had passed. Although Alderney and the other Channel Islands were surrounded by coastal forts and batteries, most of these were abandoned soon after the ending of hostilities and the garrison was reduced. In 1824 one master-gunner and two invalid gunners were listed along with the Militia as serving and maintaining the surviving Alderney defences.

After the British Government's vigorous action to suppress smuggling during the final years of the war together with the withdrawal of the garrison, economic distress in Alderney became widespread and the population fell sharply. This was further aggravated in 1825 when General John Le Mesurier surrendered his grant of the island for an annual payment of £700 from the Treasury. In an attempt to alleviate matters and at the suggestion of the Lieutenant-Governor, the common lands were divided into lots in 1830 so that island-born families would have some means of support and the inhabitants, now numbering just over a thousand, settled down to their traditional occupations of farming and fishing.

During the Restoration period, French politicians continued to argue that the coalition which had destroyed Napoleon's European empire had been transformed into a "perpetual and hostile league against France." Successive French governments had proceeded to rebuild the army and navy, to exploit divisions between the allies, secure alliances with other great powers and recover her influence in traditional spheres of Western Europe and the Mediterranean. The July revolution of 1830 and French intervention in the Belgian crisis of the same year helped to sustain the fear that France was not reconciled to the defeat and borders of 1815.

16

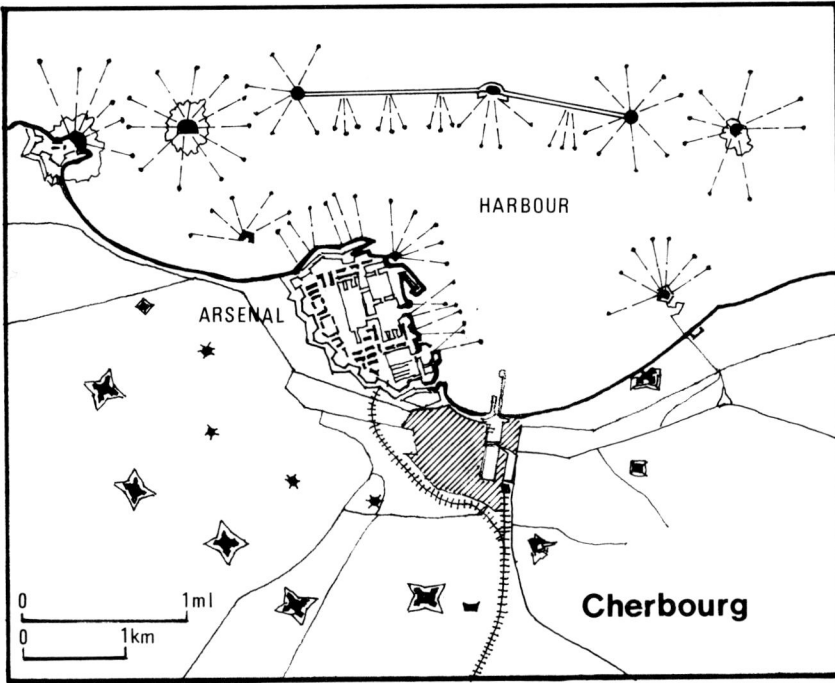

By 1858, when Queen Victoria attended the opening of the Bassin Napoleon III, the port of Cherbourg possessed a powerful chain of sea batteries and double ring of land fortifications with the new arsenal and dockyards protected by a continuous bastioned outer wall (after James Wyld).

While the Alderney people were struggling to come to terms with their economic problems, others, including the Duke of Wellington, were more concerned about the British Government's continuing neglect and reduction of military establishments like those in the Channel Islands. The duke had always held strong views regarding the Islands' military importance and of Alderney's in particular. In 1830 Colonel Cardew, Commanding Royal Engineer (CRE) Guernsey, again reported to London at some length on the need to re-fortify Alderney. His main concern was that its proximity to France would allow it to be seized at the outbreak of war before it could be garrisoned effectively. He submitted a proposal for a "Strong redoubt with a Keep" to be built on the heights of Mount Touraille; it was a fairly modest work which had barrack accommodation for less than 200 men and would mount twelve guns. The drawings are firmly inscribed "Not Approved", after rejection by the Treasury.

The potential strategic value of the island in time of war had not, however, been overlooked and over 250 vergees (101 acres) of the shoreline and land surrounding existing defence works were reserved for government use and placed in charge of the Office of Woods during the division of the common lands in 1830. Early the following year, the Alderney Militia, though reduced in numbers to some 65 gunners and 98 infantrymen, assumed a royal distinction on the King's command to coincide with the fiftieth anniversary of the defeat of Baron de Rullecourt's French forces in Jersey. While earlier efforts to enlarge the existing harbour at Alderney or create a new anchorage under the pretext of providing useful advantages for the navy had fallen on deaf ears in 1816 and again in 1826, renewed interest was now being shown in a harbour for sheltering war steamers. H. D. Inglis, in his book on the Channel Islands in 1834, noted that there had been talk of constructing a deep water harbour fit for the reception of frigates. He advocated that if the government were to seriously contemplate a naval station from which to defend the Channel trade and keep a check on Cherbourg, then it should be Alderney on which the distinction must be conferred; this was indeed a prophetic observation.

The year 1840 marked a turning point in Alderney's military history and the projection of the island from a quiet backwater into the forefront of European political rivalry. The exclusion of France from the quadripartite settlement of the crisis in the Middle East led to a breakdown in relations with Britain and the approval of a large vote in the French chambers to construct a new ring of fortifications around Paris, and to complete the harbour and arsenal at Cherbourg begun by Napoleon. The latter was viewed with considerable alarm by the Admiralty who feared for the security of the naval dockyards at Portsmouth and Plymouth, lying within easy reach of the new steam driven warships of the French navy. With the home fleet seriously undermanned and a shortage of suitable vessels for harbour protection duties, the Admiralty looked for other means to supplement the naval defence of the country. A commission of naval, artillery and engineer officers would be dispatched to the Channel Islands to identify sites for naval anchorages in each of the principal islands, these proposals receiving the consent of Sir Robert Peel's cabinet in which the aged Duke of Wellington still served.

In 1842 plans for 'Harbours of Refuge and Observation' were proposed for sites at Longis Bay in Alderney, St Catherine's Bay in Jersey and south of Terres Point in Guernsey. In the event, work did not begin in Guernsey while St Catherine's was abandoned in 1856 after only the northern breakwater had been completed. The Admiralty, however, considered Alderney to have great potential as a look-

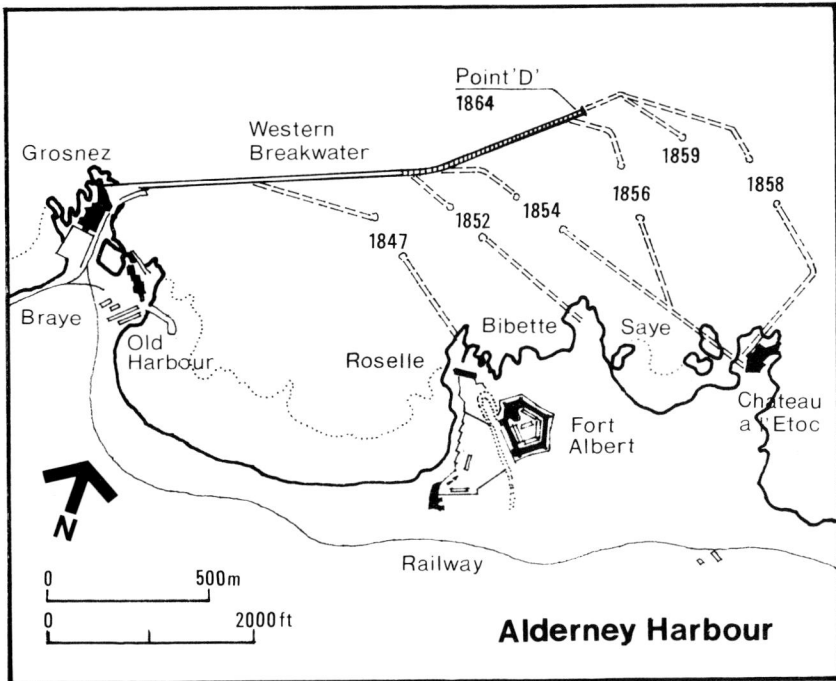

Alderney Harbour

Between 1847 and 1858 the plan for the harbour at Braye underwent progressive enlargement, while the outer section of the western breakwater (shown hatched) was allowed to collapse after 1872 and now forms a dangerous underwater reef.

out station for vessels of war and with this in mind, the proposal for a harbour at Longis was abandoned with the decision in 1844 to build it at Braye, following the report by James Walker, engineer to the Admiralty. From here a watch could be kept on the south side of the Channel, particularly on the heavily fortified port of Cherbourg 25 miles (40 km) to the east, while the new harbour at Portland might perform a similar function in the north.

While the strategic importance of a harbour in Alderney was considered to be essential for the security of British naval power in the Channel, the engineering difficulties to be encountered during the construction of the breakwater were not fully appreciated. In the Select Committee of the House of Lords' report of 1872 on the Harbour and Fortifications of Alderney is the following statement: "If such a work were now for the first time proposed, with the experience of its difficulties and results, the most eager advocate for national defences would probably hesitate in recommending its commencement."

Thomas Jackson (1808-1884) (left) and Alfred Bean (1824-1890) were the contractors for Alderney's Harbour and Victorian fortifications (T. Marchant).

Construction of the western arm of the breakwater by the contractors, Jackson and Bean, began in 1847 and continued until 1864 to the design and under the supervision of James Walker's practice. Because of the exceptional working difficulties encountered in building the masonry superstructure on its massive artificial rubble stone mound, the constant breaches by storms and the vast cost of well over £1,000,000 by the mid 1860s, the work is well documented in reports to parliament and the annual debates preceding the recurring votes. The anchorage was originally designed as embracing between two breakwaters an area of 67 acres; this was progressively increased until by 1858 it was planned to be 150 acres in area with a minimum depth of three fathoms (5.5 m). The work proceeded rapidly at first with the western arm reaching 900 yards (823 m) from the shore by 1856, but from here the work became much more laborious as the depth of water increased. By 1864 the head of the breakwater had reached 1,600 yards (1463 m) from the shore in a depth of over 130 feet (38 m) of water at low tide, and no further new construction was undertaken as the harbour was still not big enough for warships of the tonnage by then contemplated. Construction of the eastern arm was not carried through, and the harbour consequently never fulfilled its purpose.

The stone-faced inner harbour was constructed between 1847 and 1849 to shelter the hopper barges, steam tugs and other craft engaged in building the breakwater. These barges were loaded with stone brought from Mannez Quarry by the mineral railway laid down for this purpose and which is still in use today. Behind the Hammond Memorial a cutting can still be seen, which was the route for the former branch line, via the embankment and arch at Arch Bay, to the proposed eastern breakwater at Fort Château à L'Étoc.

In 1847, the year in which construction of the harbour commenced, Sir John Burgoyne, the Inspector-General of Fortifications (IGF) wrote a memorandum on the defenceless state of the country should war break out with France. Lord Palmerston, now foreign secretary in Lord John Russell's administration, drew up a report with the aid of Sir John which was laid before the cabinet. It pointed out that France, although inferior as a naval power, might by her better organised system of naval preparation or by manoeuvres, make herself superior in the Channel for up to two weeks. During that time, having an immensely superior army, she might land any number of men she chose and destroy the dockyards thus paralysing British naval resources for years. The report went on to propose that £6,000,000 should be spent on fortifying the dockyards both on their sea and land fronts and to provide "great harbours as stations for our fleet."

However, it was not until Louis Napoleon's coup d'état in 1852 and the foundation of the Second Empire, that Russell's government determined to improve the defences of the country and so render invasion impossible. It was at this time that the main phase of construction of the forts and breakwater in Alderney was proceeding, and from 1854 to 1858 the size of the proposed harbour increased almost yearly.

Although the construction of the western breakwater continued for over 25 years, the building of the chain of eighteen separate forts and batteries proceeded relatively quickly, though not without many policy changes. Originally, in 1842, a single fort on Essex Hill was to be the only 'sovereign work' to defend the harbour proposed for Longis Bay. With the decision to construct the harbour at Braye, additional works were proposed and it was suggested that Longis should be sealed completely with a breakwater. These proposals, in 1847, were for a new sovereign work on Les Rochers, a redoubt at Butes, a tower on Essex Hill and additional works detailed for Mount Touraille, Roselle and Grosnez points, together with a heavy battery at the end of the breakwater. The Board of Ordnance then informed the IGF that the Treasury had voted money to purchase the land. By 1848 there were proposals to build round towers at Grosnez, Château à L'Étoc, Rat (sic) Island and Clonque, but after a visit by the IGF and the Master-General of the Ordnance these were abandoned.

In April 1850, after numerous changes in policy and with many more to come, the Board of Ordnance finally gave its authority to begin work on the first fort at Grosnez at the landward end of the new western breakwater. The succeeding chain of forts and batteries which so dominate Alderney's landscape today, was then constructed rapidly between 1850 and 1859. It extends from Fort Clonque in the

Captain (later Major-General Sir) William F. D. Jervois, GCMG, CB, began his distinguished career as Britain's foremost military engineer of the nineteenth century with his work on the fortifications of Alderney (J. Jervois).

west, around the north and east coasts of the island to Essex Barracks and Longis Lines. Although construction continued throughout this period, it is possible to recognise three overlapping phases in this impressive undertaking.

The first phase, that of building Fort Grosnez, resulted from the immediate need to afford protection to the inner harbour and its facilities during the initial stage of the breakwater construction. The engineer in charge was Lieutenant F.C. Hassard, who came from the Guernsey depot of the Royal Engineers where he had been acting CRE. With the exception of Fort Albert, the Arsenal and Mount Hale Battery, all the other forts and batteries were constructed during the second phase. The construction of Fort Albert and the Arsenal complex was a late decision taken in 1855 and may be recognised as the third phase in the fortification of Alderney.

By early 1851, with the construction of Fort Grosnez under way and a major programme of fortification about to be embarked upon, the CRE Guernsey made an urgent request to the Board of Ordnance for a captain of engineers to supervise the intended works. In June 1852, Captain William F. D. Jervois, who was commanding a company of Sappers and Miners at Woolwich, was ordered to Alderney with his company. Recently married, he first expressed interest in an alternative posting and was accordingly ordered to Brighton. However, after reading a report by Sir John Burgoyne expressing the belief that Alderney was as important to Britain as Gibraltar, the ambitious Captain Jervois begged to have his orders rescinded and so went as originally intended to Alderney. This move had great influence on his distinguished career, particularly in securing his appointment as secretary to the 1859 Royal Commission on the Defences of the United Kingdom. From 1852 until their completion in 1859, Jervois was responsible for the design of the Alderney forts and supervised their construction.

The British fleet manoeuvres of 1890 gave islanders a rare opportunity of seeing how Alderney Harbour might have acted in time of war with France (Priaulx Library).

The commencement of these important government works focused European attention on the most northerly Channel Island for more than a quarter of a century, during which time Alderney prospered at the expense of its larger neighbours. The whole infrastructure of the island was transformed with the influx of labour engaged in the construction of the harbour and fortifications and the arrival of British garrison forces. The town expanded, many new shops opened and the principal public buildings — the Court House, the gaol, the Anglican church and Methodist chapel — were built at this time. Queen Victoria visited Alderney on three occasions in 1854, 1857 and 1859, giving Prince Albert the opportunity to inspect the works of defence in which he had taken such a close interest through correspondence and discussion with the principal officers of the Ordnance and leading politicians.

The second half of the nineteenth century was to see the warship and the power of the weapons with which it was armed — and therefore those of coastal artillery — increase to an extent that was inconceivable in the 1850s. Alderney's forts would be unlikely to survive shelling from the new rifled guns and its harbour was of insufficient size to hold a fleet of ironclads. The Royal Navy was to use the harbour on only two occasions for the summer manoeuvres of the Home Fleet in 1890 and 1901.

The 1872 report from the Select Committee of the House of Lords on the Harbour and Fortifications of Alderney stated that the total cost of the breakwater to date had been over one and a half million pounds. There was general agreement amongst military and naval officers that the harbour would be of great service in the event of war and should not be allowed to fall into an enemy's hands, and the cabinet decided in the following year to maintain the breakwater. From the harbour, small vessels could watch the Channel, protect Britain's trade and oppose vessels of the enemy. Jervois, who was called to give evidence, stated that modern improvements in artillery would induce him to suggest that two forts would be sufficient to prevent the island being seized by an enemy. Within the space of twenty years, the man who had designed the principal works for the defence of Alderney was obliged to concede that they were already obsolete; such was the progress in the development of armament and tactical thinking in the latter half of the century. Even though they were outdated, most of the larger forts were still armed until the end of the century, but with fewer guns. The armament consisted of a mixture of smooth-bore (SB) and rifled muzzle-loading (RML) guns and after 1885 some rifled breech-loading (RBL) guns.

In 1886, the newly constituted Royal Artillery and Royal Engineer Works Committee, noting the government's commitment to the maintenance of the breakwater, proposed to revise the armament for Alderney and to concentrate the defence in Fort Albert, allowing the other forts to be dismantled. The decision by the Joint Naval and Military Committee on Defence, that Alderney would be a useful station for torpedo-craft in time of war, assured its status as a defended port in 1891.

At the turn of the century, with the rationalisation of coast defence ordnance, Fort Albert was re-armed in 1901 with two 6-inch BL guns while two 12-pounder quick-firing (QF) guns were installed at Roselle Battery along with two defence electric lights. The installation of these guns marked the beginning of the final phase of British military interest in Alderney.

The social consequences of the mid-nineteenth century influx of English and Irish labourers and their subsequent disappearance in the 1870s were dramatic. Having recovered from the depression which followed the withdrawal of the garrison at the end of the Napoleonic Wars, the inhabitants once again suffered economic distress, appealing to the government to hand over and support the quarrying industry which had developed for the export of crushed stone.

With the rise of German naval power after 1905, the defended ports of the United Kingdom were reassessed to determine the scale of attack which they might be expected to meet. Successive Alderney

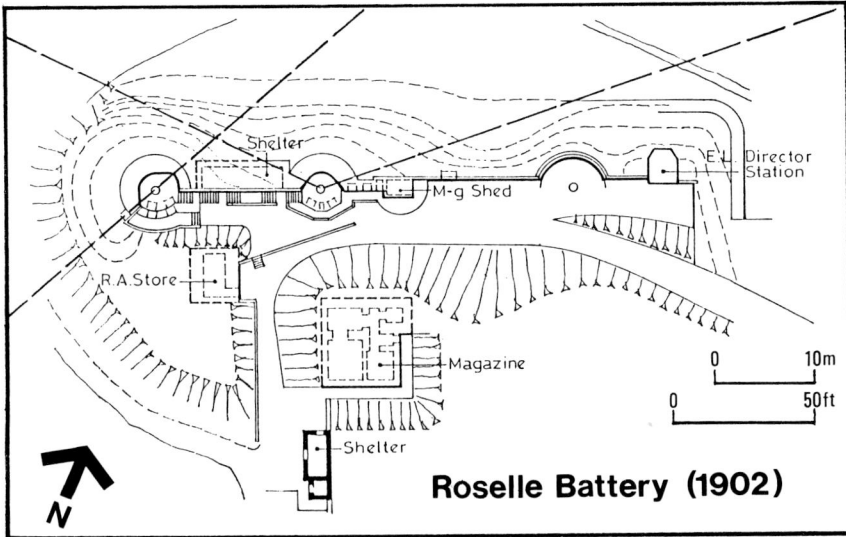

Roselle Battery (1902)

defence schemes were prepared by the War Office before the outbreak of the First World War to lay down the necessary war establishment and the measures to be taken on the commencement of hostilities, including the preparation of some fifty defensive fieldworks with positions for mobile armament. The fixed armament at Fort Albert and Roselle Point was manned by Militia gunners. A new octagonal concrete pillbox was constructed to cover the defence electric lights at Roselle, and the Port War Signal Station was sited at Essex Hill to provide radio communications with the other islands.

The coastal defences of the Channel Islands were never put to the test during the Great War. The harbour at Alderney made no contribution to the naval defence of the country, and in 1921 the Admiralty finally abandoned all claim to its usefulness, handing over the maintenance of the breakwater to civilian contractors following several years of acrimonious and protracted negotiations. In 1925, the Committee of Imperial Defence referred the question of the strategic value of the Channel Islands to the Chiefs of Staff who recommended the withdrawal of the garrison of regular troops. When the government adopted the proposal that the Army should no longer bear any charge in connection with the Islands' militia forces in 1928, the end of Alderney's coastal defence was signalled. The following year, the Alderney Militia was disbanded and the guns removed from Fort Albert and Roselle Battery. During the 1930s, the War Department began the sale of the smaller Victorian forts and batteries by public auction, finally handing over the larger works to the States.

The events which led to the German invasion and occupation of the Channel Islands during the Second World War and the subsequent sufferings of the islanders are well documented. Accounts of the German occupation of Alderney have always been exposed to unique difficulties. Virtually all the inhabitants were evacuated in June 1940, and also for many years there has been speculation on alleged atrocities committed against the forced labourers. The most authoritative account of conditions in Alderney was compiled by Major 'Bunny' Pantcheff, the military intelligence officer sent by the War Office after liberation to investigate the allegations of atrocities and mass murders. He refutes both the accusations of a 'cover-up' by the British and many of the allegations of the more inhuman practices supposedly carried out in Alderney. His conclusions are based on his interrogation in 1945 of the whole German garrison and those of the prisoners and civilian labourers who remained. Nevertheless, he emphasises that the forced labourers were brutally treated and that the inmates of *Lager Sylt*, the only concentration camp in the Channel Islands, suffered the utmost degradation.

The period between the outbreak of the war and the capitulation of France was one of utter confusion. Soon after the Great War the British Government had come to the conclusion that the Channel Islands were of little strategic value, and that to defend them would serve no military purpose. Although a battalion of troops did remain in Guernsey until 1939 the garrison was withdrawn from Jersey. In June 1940, with the German armies advancing westwards, the Chiefs of Staff decided that certain token defensive measures should be taken in Jersey and Guernsey. However, the plan to send two more battalions was cancelled as the enemy approached the Channel coast and the remaining British forces were quickly withdrawn.

Military evacuation was completed by 21 June, and it was expected that the Foreign Office would inform the German Government that the Islands had been demilitarised. However, the Home Office withheld the press notice to this effect on the grounds that it would effectively be an invitation to the Germans to invade. After attempting for ten days to establish if the Islands were defended, the *Luftwaffe* bombed St Helier and St Peter Port on 28 June killing 44 civilians. Only now did the British Government belatedly inform the Germans that the Islands had been demilitarised.

As these momentous events were unfolding in the other islands, the inhabitants of Alderney were becoming more uneasy. The only official means of communication with the outside world was by a single radio telephone in the post office and this was seriously affected by a government order to observe strict radio silence. The islanders felt defenceless and abandoned, and the inevitable decision to evacuate

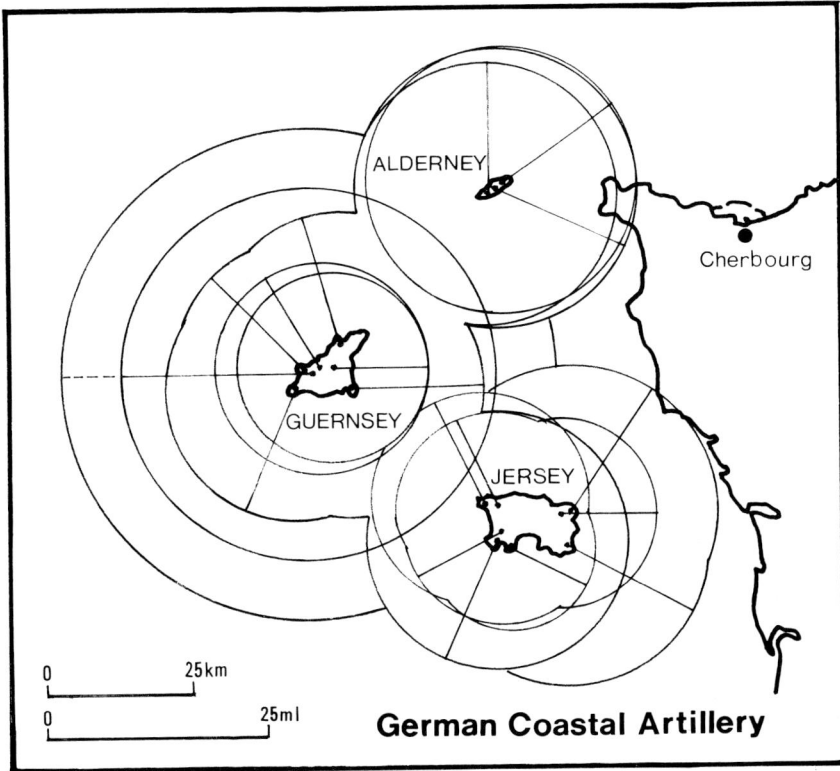

ALDERNEY

Cherbourg

GUERNSEY

JERSEY

| 0 | 25km |
| 0 | 25ml |

German Coastal Artillery

was reluctantly taken on 22 June at a public meeting on the Butes. The following day, with a few exceptions, the inhabitants embarked on ships sent from England and Alderney was left to its fate.

Assuming the Channel Islands to be defended, the invasion had been planned with some caution by the Germans under the code name Operation 'Green Arrow', but the absence of any visible signs of surrender led to the bombing of St Helier and St Peter Port on 28 June. Two days later a *Luftwaffe* pilot carrying out a routine reconnaissance, on observing that the Guernsey airfield was deserted, landed and established that the island was undefended. Thus the enterprise of one pilot resulted in a few red faces amongst the German commanders who were forced to hastily revise their plans for the occupation. For all practical purposes, Guernsey was occupied on 30 June and Jersey surrendered the next day. On 2 July, two light aircraft landed on the obstructed airstrip in Alderney and cleared the runway. Finally, on 4 July, a small detachment of troops crossed to Sark from Guernsey and the initial occupation was complete.

The occupation and subsequent fortification of the Channel Islands has always been considered to be entirely due to Hitler's personal obsession with the possession of British soil. Undoubtedly, the occupation was of great propaganda value to the Germans, and if the invasion of Britain under the code name Operation 'Sealion' had gone ahead, the Islands would certainly have had some part to play. However, with the failure of the *Luftwaffe* to gain air superiority during the Battle of Britain — a prerequisite for invasion — 'Sealion' was indefinitely postponed while Hitler sought to reduce Britain by other means. In early 1941, submarine bases were established in France and, due to the initial success of the U-boat campaign, Operation 'Barbarossa' — the invasion of Russia — commenced in June.

As Hitler's thoughts turned from Britain towards the Soviet Union, he issued a series of instructions for the strengthening of the Channel Islands' defences. In his directive of 20 October 1941, it was laid down that the Islands were to be turned into an impregnable fortress. Already the 319 Infantry Division together with anti-aircraft units had been committed in June in anticipation of a British attempt to recover the Islands.

Prior to the postponement of 'Sealion' and the invasion of Russia, Hitler had never envisaged a static defensive front in the west, but after the Japanese attack on the American Pacific fleet at Pearl Harbor in December 1941, the occupied territories were placed in greater danger by rallying American aid for Britain. Consequently, Hitler issued further directives for the installation of permanent garrisons to defend the continental coastline. Throughout 1942 plans were formulated for the construction of a 'new West Wall', comprising permanent concrete fortifications and heavy artillery batteries, which would defend the whole of the coastline of occupied Europe from Norway to the Spanish frontier. Hitler planned this 'Atlantic Wall' to have 15,000 strongpoints and to be defended by 300,000 troops. The proposed programme listed the defences in order of importance as ports for coastal traffic, ports suitable for enemy use, the Channel Islands and possible landing places on the open coast. Thus was started one of the most impressive fortification construction programmes that the world had ever seen.

The fortification of the Channel Islands was conducted in three distinct phases. The relatively inactive period between occupation and Hitler's directive of October 1941 constitutes the first phase, during which few defences were constructed in Alderney apart from a small number of infantry strongpoints, the reinforcing of some of the Victorian forts and the emplacement of some light anti-aircraft batteries. Throughout 1941 the Germans were mainly concerned with maintaining the breakwater, cleaning up the island and determining if crops could be grown successfully to supplement Guernsey's civilian foodstocks. This relatively quiet period came to an end with the arrival of the Organization Todt and continued through the main construction phase in 1942 and 1943. Finally, there was the period of gradual run-down in construction due to the diminishing supply of building materials after the eventual withdrawal of the labourers to the continent by June 1944.

Although far smaller in area than either Jersey or Guernsey, Alderney was fortified to a greater degree than the other islands, having thirteen infantry strongpoints and twelve resistance nests, five coastal artillery batteries and twenty-one anti-aircraft batteries. Throughout 1942 and 1943, construction of the permanent defences continued with great intensity, reaching its height in September 1943. By October, the supply of cement and structural steel for the Islands had begun to dwindle with a corresponding and progressive withdrawal of the labour force.

By the beginning of 1944, Hitler had established combat zones for the expected invasion of Europe and, in February, the Channel Islands were added to the twelve designated 'Fortresses' that were to be defended to the last man. However, after the Normandy landings in June 1944, it soon became obvious that the Allies had no intention of assaulting the Islands, but hoped to force their capitulation by isolating them and so cutting off their supplies. On 9 May 1945, the German forces in Guernsey and Jersey finally surrendered, but it was not until 16 May that British troops of Task Force 135 formally repossessed Alderney. Soon after, more than two thousand prisoners of war were shipped out, but a working force remained to begin the massive programme of clearance of matériel, including the extensive minefields, from the island. Much of the hardware of occupation — small arms, ammunition, artillery and tanks — was dumped into the Hurd Deep, north of Alderney. Fixed armaments remained for some years, only to be cleared finally in one of the many post-war scrap drives. It was not until seven months later, on 2 December, that the first group of islanders was allowed to return to Alderney, five and a half years after evacuation; this happy, but traumatic return is admirably described in *The Alderney Story: 1939-1949*.

Today, the visitor to Alderney is only too aware of the many works of defence which bear testimony to its strategic importance at various intervals, extending over some two thousand years. These impressive fortifications are stark reminders of man's desire for protection against the threat of invasion. The German works, representing the last phase in the island's military history are, at the same time, permanent memorials to those who suffered and died in their construction.

2. A PRECARIOUS EXISTENCE

The French Revolutionary and Napoleonic Wars

At the outbreak of the French Revolutionary Wars, Alderney's eighteenth century defences were in a dilapidated and inefficient state. The open batteries recommended to the Board of Ordnance in 1739 by Colonel Bastide were simple earthwork positions, not all with stone platforms for the guns and, with few exceptions, were overbuilt by later works. None of these earlier sites is in evidence today.

With little change in design of warships and artillery for land and sea service during the second half of the century, apart from the introduction of the carronade, the requirements for coastal defence remained unchanged. When Governor Peter Le Mesurier detailed the problems of manning the surviving batteries and requested heavier guns for the defence of Crabby in 1794, these were despatched immediately and the Commanding Royal Engineer in Guernsey was ordered to carry out an immediate inspection. In common with the procedure for assessing the defences of the United Kingdom, the War Office divided the coastline into twelve districts each under the command of a general officer who instructed the senior RE officer to submit reports and recommendations to the Board of Ordnance for the improvement of local defences.

When the Inspector-General of Fortifications called for a report on the Alderney defences in 1801, the island possessed just 48 guns on standing carriages and a further fifteen on field carriages, the disposition of which was the cause of a serious dispute between the Governor and the senior officer appointed to command the troops, Brigadier-General Este. Peter Le Mesurier strongly opposed the dismantling of five batteries on the shoreline and the withdrawal of their armament to batteries on higher ground.

After a survey of the existing works had been made, the first of a series of comprehensive reports with recommendations was submitted to the Master-General of the Ordnance (MGO) by Lieutenant-Colonel Mackelcan, CRE, in late 1802. This showed an increase in the number of guns mounted in the island's nineteen effective batteries to some 85 pieces. These included the retired works at York Hill and Stoney Hill, King's and Mannez Batteries, and Kent and Clarence Batteries below Essex. Le Mesurier rightly considered Kent and Clarence Batteries superfluous in opposing ships, especially at night, and a danger to gunners manning batteries in advanced positions, not least from their exposure to falling wadding from guns in the rear. Only five of the batteries possessed furnaces for heating shot, an essential adjunct to artillery firing against wooden warships of the day in an attempt to

John Le Mesurier,
GOVERNOR OF ALDERNEY.

*La première chose qu'on doit faire quand on a emprunté un
Livre, c'est de le lire afin de pouvoir le rendre plutôt*

Menagiana Vol.4.

The coat of arms of the Governor, John Le Mesurier, reflects the determination
of successive generations to protect their island heritage (Jacob's Annals).

disable or destroy them before they could reach a position close
enough to the shore to disembark a landing force in small boats.
Mackelcan was concerned primarily with the efficiency of the armament
of the batteries, proposing to retain 26 of the heavier guns mounted
and ready for immediate service, to place all of the carronades and
brass ordnance in store and to withdraw the remaining heavy guns
and all of the 9-pounders from those batteries considered superfluous.
These latter works were to be retained for infantry or field artillery
positions, but not maintained.

Of equal concern to the Board of Ordnance was the provision of
secure storehouses and magazines for the artillery stores and ammunition. Few of these were owned by the Board of Ordnance, most
having been either erected by the States of Alderney for the service
or hired for the purpose. Similarly, barrack accommodation was at a
premium, with the garrison force of 446 men of the five companies of
Royal Invalids to house, supported by 194 rank and file of the
Militia. In an attempt to ease the problem of rented accommodation,
the Board had approved the construction of a new barracks in 1801 at
Clonque, the ruins of which are still visible on the Zig-Zag, and at
Corblets and Longis, both of which still survive in part to this day.

After a brief, peaceful interlude, the resumption of hostilities between England and France in 1803 brought fresh anxieties to those concerned with the state of Alderney's security. This turn of events coincided with the appointment of Major-General (later Lieutenant-General, Sir) John Doyle as the Lieutenant-Governor of Guernsey who, as an officer of great zeal, devoted his energies to the improvement of the defences of the Bailiwick. In particular, he recognised the need for a permanent work in Alderney as a place of arms to which the defending forces could retire, if necessary until relieved, and supported the opinion expressed as early as 1799 that Mount Touraille should be the site for such a work. His remarks were founded on reports prepared in May 1804 by Lieutenant (later General) G. Cardew, RE, and Brigadier-General J. Brodrick.

Both Cardew and Brodrick pointed to the number of batteries which were poorly sited, of weak construction, incapable of being defended and which led to the dispersal of the forces manning them. The expense of maintaining these works, they concluded, would be better charged in the construction of permanent works at Touraille and Essex, capable of mutual support and command of the vulnerable eastern end of the island as well as Braye Bay. Nothing less than these works would enable the defending troops to resist an attacking force if driven back from the shore batteries. With the renewed threat of invasion, Alderney was now reinforced with detachments of the 5th Royal Veterans Battalion and 57th Regiment in support of the island's Militia whose competence as artillerymen was well recognised.

Improved naval security after the French defeats of 1805 did little to diminish the Lieutenant-Governor's call for maintaining the island's defences which were considered in "a respectable state" by the end of the year. Doyle continued to press the government for funds to construct a place of arms, plans and estimates having been prepared for top-lit casemates supporting a terreplein for a battery of guns around a tower, surmounted by a single gun, and containing two internal floors above a magazine and cistern. The plans were never sanctioned and a return of the ordnance in 1806 showed that a total of 93 guns remained serviceable in nineteen batteries in spite of Colonel Mackelcan's recommendations, while the Militia rank and file had been increased to 339 men. At the same time, the Home Office had approved the full-time employment of one man at the rate of 10d per day to maintain the fortifications in a constant state of repair.

By 1809, the Channel Islands had again come under threat of invasion whereupon Sir John Doyle renewed his plea to Lord Castlereagh for the erection of a place of arms at Mount Touraille,

This drawing of 1810, while exhibiting a certain topographical licence, clearly shows the remnants of Essex Castle on the skyline with distant watch houses and from left to right, the guard house at Longis Lines, the soldiers' and officers' quarters at Longis Barracks, and the former Essex Barracks at the extreme right (Priaulx Library).

two Sussex towers and various improvements to the batteries based on a modified version of earlier proposals in order to reduce the probable expenditure. Although General Morse, IGF, was instructed to appoint a committee of Royal Engineer officers to examine the defences of the Channel Islands, no orders were given to include Alderney. Sir John continued to deprecate the government's desire for economy and apparent disregard for the plight of Alderney. He strongly criticised the Board of Ordnance, and the Inspector-General in particular, for not having acted upon the reports submitted by successive engineers. In reply, General Morse expressed the belief that France would never make a separate attack on Alderney and that the provision of any other works, other than shore batteries, would be unnecessary; he also noted the difference of opinion between the Lieutenant-Governor and the new CRE over the site for a proposed place of arms. Out of sheer frustration over the Board's inaction, Sir John attempted to collect masons and artificers from Guernsey to bolster the labour force in Alderney. He also authorised the expenditure of £500 from his own purse to implement the most pressing works, taking care to call for accounts in triplicate "as the auditors are quite as formidable as the French." Representations were also being made by Admiral Phillippe d'Auvergne to extend the experimental French telegraphic system within the Islands to include Alderney as the advanced position watching enemy vessels sailing out of Cherbourg.

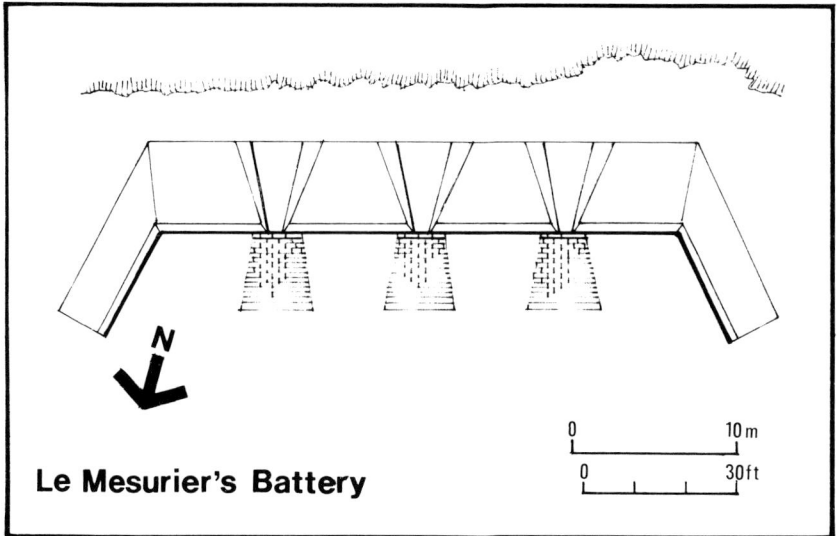

Le Mesurier's Battery

0   10 m

0   30 ft

The first of two reports prepared in 1810 by Lieutenant-Colonel De Butts, CRE, had detailed the works which were still considered necessary to complete the defences of Alderney, and attached to them was a statement of the essential improvements and repairs to the existing batteries. While the round towers which he proposed for the centre of Platte Saline, Rat Island and Quesnard, with a bastioned place of arms at Les Rochers were never adopted, certain new works were approved and constructed in the ensuing years in accordance with the recommendations contained in the supplementary report prepared by Captain Hutcheson, RA, in September 1811.

Batteries

When Mackelcan carried out his inspection of the Alderney defences in 1802, 25 of the island's 85 guns were concentrated in six batteries fringing the shoreline and slopes of Essex Hill to command the only sheltered anchorage at Longis Bay. Kent and Clarence Batteries, known as the Queen's Lines, were sited halfway up the slope of Essex Hill and these positions can be clearly seen as level terraces, though overgrown, especially when the shadows lengthen in the afternoon sun. Prince of Wales Battery with its extreme, southerly projecting gun position still known as Frying Pan Battery, was an extension of the original Longis Lines at shore level although lacking a masonry scarp at this date. A two-gun battery, just to the east of the Nunnery and sometimes referred to as Revelard Battery completed the defences of Longis Bay at the turn of the century.

34

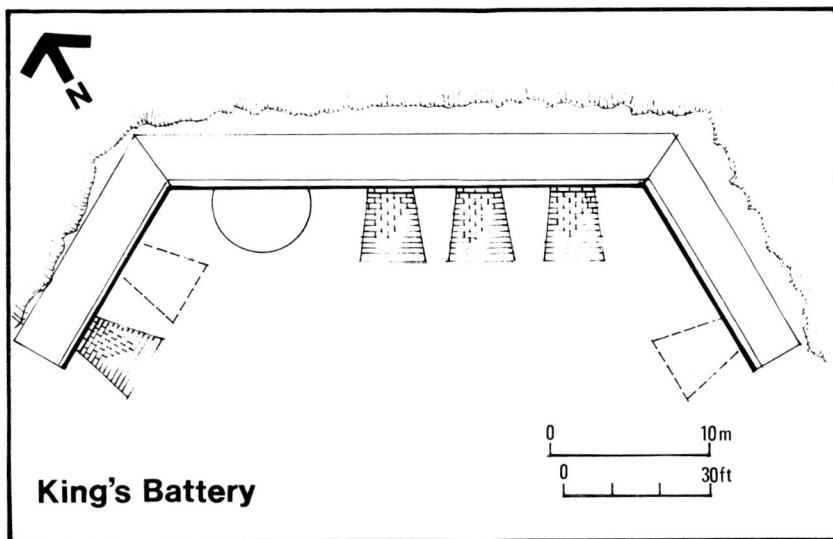

King's Battery

0 _____ 10 m

0 _____ 30 ft

In the consolidation of the defences in this area which occurred from 1804 onwards under Sir John Doyle's hand, Kent and Clarence Batteries were dismantled and fifteen guns mounted at the shore with a shot furnace in the reconstituted Longis Lines. The battery beside the Nunnery was retained and a new three-gun battery, Le Mesurier's, was constructed in the centre of the bay to command the approaches. By 1816 the number of guns in Longis Lines had been reduced to just ten pieces and the Nunnery battery dismantled.

The eastern extremity of the island had traditionally been lightly defended, the dangerous rocks and tides providing a degree of natural protection. But acknowledging the experience of local pilots, Captain Hutcheson's recommendations of 1811 were adopted to strengthen the battery at Canard Point (known now as Quesnard) and to mount five guns close to the position where ships approaching from Cherbourg must pass. The older gun positions on higher ground at Mannez and beside the adjoining guardhouse were then dismantled.

The protection of Corblets and Saye Bays was afforded by a strengthened earlier battery at Chateau à L'Etoc, supported by retired batteries on high ground at King's and Stoney Hill, the principal work being King's Battery with seven guns and a furnace for heating shot. An additional two-gun battery was built on the shoreline in the centre of Saye Bay in 1811.

The wide expanse of Braye Bay called for two salient positions at Braye itself and Roselle Point, with a central position at Roquelais, named Elizabeth Battery in 1804 with the mounting of six guns on

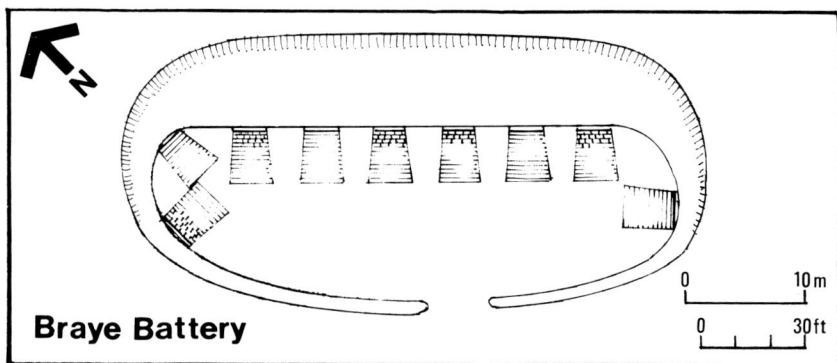

Braye Battery

0   10 m

0   30 ft

stone platforms half way up the slopes to Les Rochers. This position
was later moved closer to the shoreline, designed to mount nine guns
and renamed St Anne's Battery. The battery at Braye, reduced to
eight guns in 1811, and the five-gun battery at Roselle Point secured
the approaches. All three batteries had been equipped with furnaces
for heating shot in 1806, while a battery of three guns adjoining a
guardhouse at Mount Touraille to the east of Braye Bay, and known
as Fahy's, was dismantled at this time.

The salient position of Grosnez Point had provided the site for an
earlier battery to protect Crabby Bay and Little Crabby to the west
and east respectively and, while this was retained for three guns, a
much larger elevated and retired battery of fourteen guns on York
Hill had been constructed during the French Revolutionary War
period, to which was added a furnace in 1806. By 1816, however, this
battery had been disarmed, its purpose having been superceded by a
new four-gun battery at Doyle's Point formerly known as Houmet
Battery, and the improvement of the armament at Grosnez and
Braye Batteries.

The height of Rocque Tourgie, commanding Clonque Bay to the
west and Platte Saline to the east, and the Lines of Jefonie (known
now as the Giffoine) had been the sites for two small batteries in
1802 and the only works of defence at the western extremity of the
island. The vulnerability of Platte Saline was identified by Captain
Hutcheson in his report of 1811 and the original battery of four guns
in the centre of the bay dates from this time. Ordnance had been
mounted adjoining the barracks at Clonque in 1806, but this position
was not strengthened to mount four guns until Hutcheson had formulated his recommendations. This is the only battery position from
the Napoleonic period which can be traced on the ground, the others
having been mostly overbuilt by the Victorian works or lost through
quarrying.

36

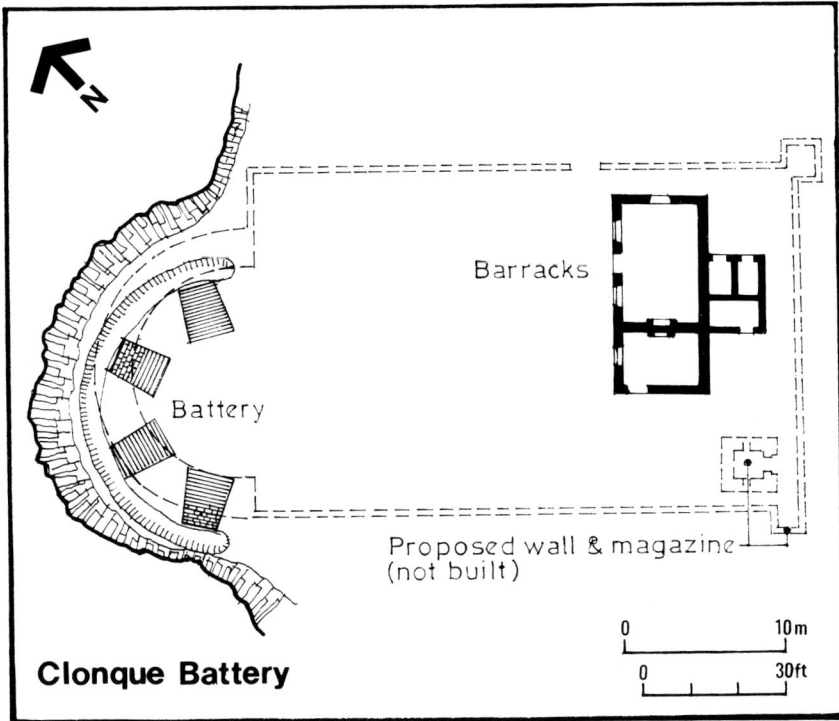

N

Barracks

Battery

Proposed wall & magazine
(not built)

0   10 m

0   30 ft

Clonque Battery

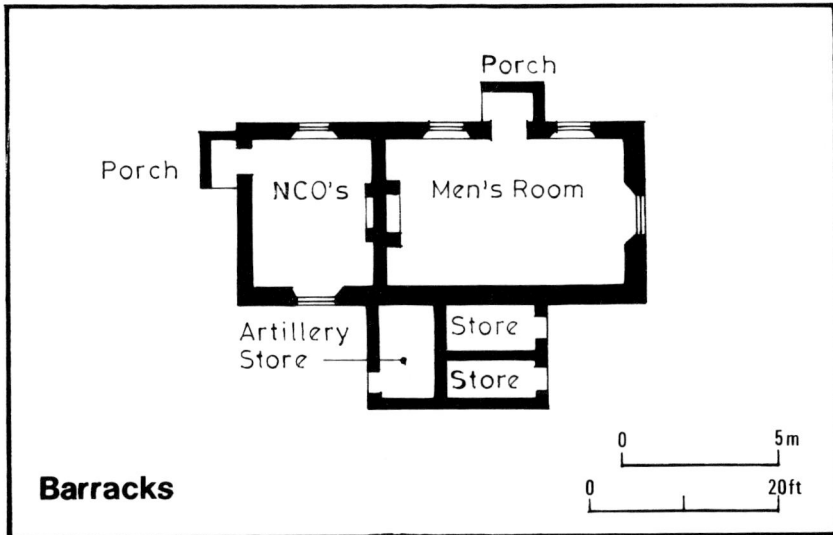

Porch

Porch

NCO's   Men's Room

Artillery
Store

Store

Store

0   5 m

0   20 ft

Barracks

By 1816, the number of batteries in Alderney had been reduced to fifteen, mounting a total of 70 guns. With the coming of peace, the ordnance was dismounted so that within ten years just eighteen guns remained in place, the others having been taken into store, while the batteries themselves soon fell into a ruinous condition through lack of maintenance.

The 1830 project for a place of arms, called for by the Master-General of the Ordnance and submitted by the CRE Guernsey, Lieutenant-Colonel George Cardew, was intended to provide accommodation for at least 200 men with artillery, and all the stores, ammunition, provisions and water required to enable them to hold out against a superior force until relieved and to be situated in a place capable of protecting the disembarkation of the relieving force. Cardew recommended Mount Touraille as the site in preference to Les Rochers and Fort or Essex Hill, and drawings were prepared by John Wilson. Although the Treasury found that no case had been justified for the construction of this work, the plans are of some interest.

They show a regular work of modest scale suited to the pronounced conical form of the hill at that time and before it was substantially cut down to the level upon which the present Fort Albert stands. Approached from the north-east by a drawbridge crossing a ditch on this and the south-east face only, the redoubt was square in plan with two bastions at opposite salients and a wide terreplein mounting eight guns *en barbette*. The 20 feet (6m) wide ditch was flanked by two casemated counterscarp galleries with underground access. The north-west and south-west faces of the redoubt were deemed to be protected by the ground which fell steeply away to the shoreline.

The square keep, comprising three floors of storage and barrack accommodation with mountings for four guns on its roof, was loopholed for musketry on all four sides. The base of each wall was afforded some measure of protection by four machicoulis, one in the centre of each face. A well some 160 feet (49m) deep was to be sunk within the work. Four internal light wells provided light and air to the barracks.

Other Works

The earliest reports made during the Napoleonic period had not only called for improvements to the coast batteries in Alderney, but also for the provision of proper magazines and storehouses which were well protected and accessible. Detached magazines which remained in use up to 1816 and beyond were sited at the Nunnery, York Hill and Platte Saline, while smaller storehouses were built at Longis Lines, Corblets, King's, Braye and Roselle by the Ordnance Department.

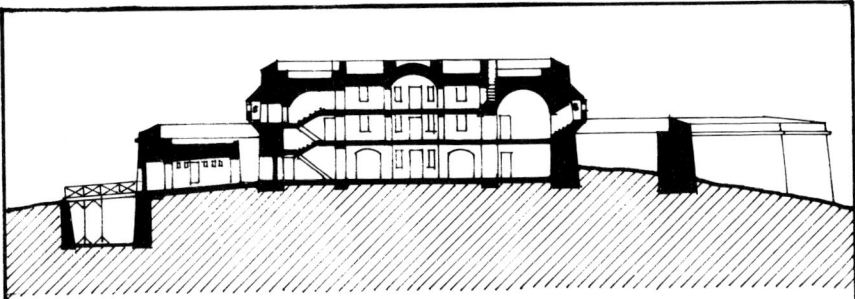

Section

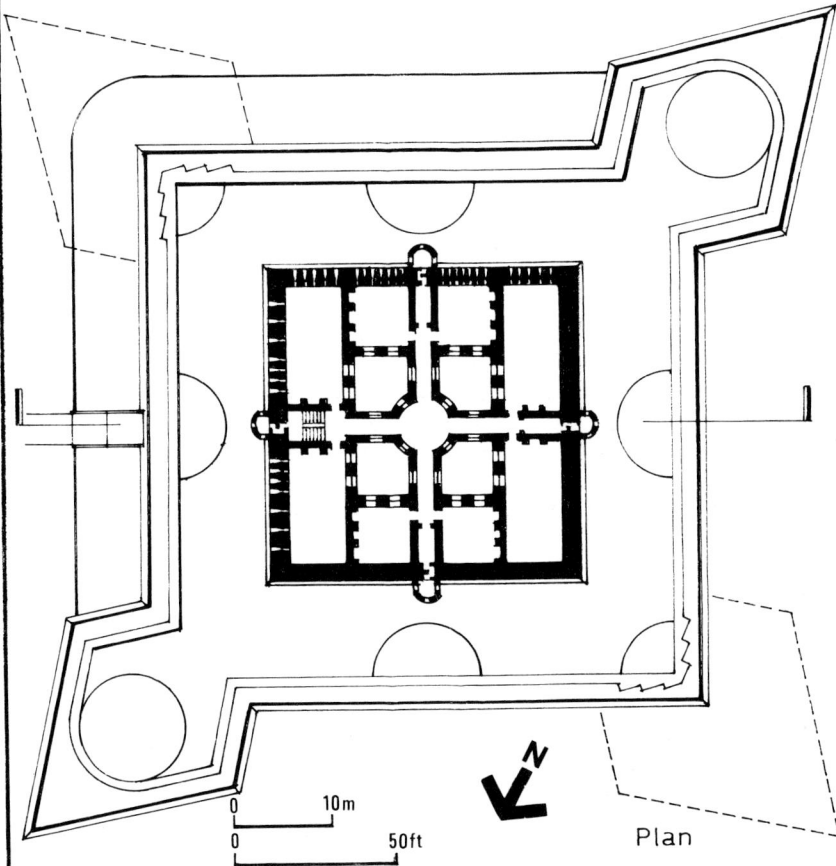

0   10m

0   50ft

Plan

Project for a Place of Arms, Mount Touraille, 1830 (not built)

Les Rochers

1   2   3   4   5   6   7

1. Platte Saline   4. Braye   7. Longis Lines
2. York Hill   5. King's
3. Roselle   6. Corblets

Magazines

0 _____ 10m

0 _____ 30ft

The Ordnance Storekeeper's house and yard were in High Street.

In 1810 the Board of Ordnance issued orders for the purchase of land at Les Rochers from the States for the construction of two new magazines within walled enclosures. Construction proceeded early the following year of a 200 barrel powder magazine with a detached shifting room to the west, and a smaller magazine for fixed ammunition to the east. The latter of these two stone buildings is still intact, and its pitched roof forms a prominent feature of the property known appropriately as 'The Armoury'.

The States of Alderney also made land available at the Butes in 1813 to the Ordnance Department for the construction of a barrack and storehouses for the Royal Artillery. They adjoin the wide elevated expanse of the exercise ground traditionally used by the line regiments on ceremonial occasions and as the principal assembly point for the Alderney Militia. Built round a central yard with underground water storage, the south-west range of buildings comprised the carriage sheds and guard room, with the NCOs' room and barracks for 28 men and cookhouse opposite; the shot store formed the north-east range, with coal store and privies. Converted later in the century for use as a hospital with adjoining gunshed, some parts remain, though much altered, to give an impression of its original appearance. It is now occupied by the Public Works department. The Signal House built just to the east of the Royal Artillery Barracks at the same period, was demolished in the 1830s.

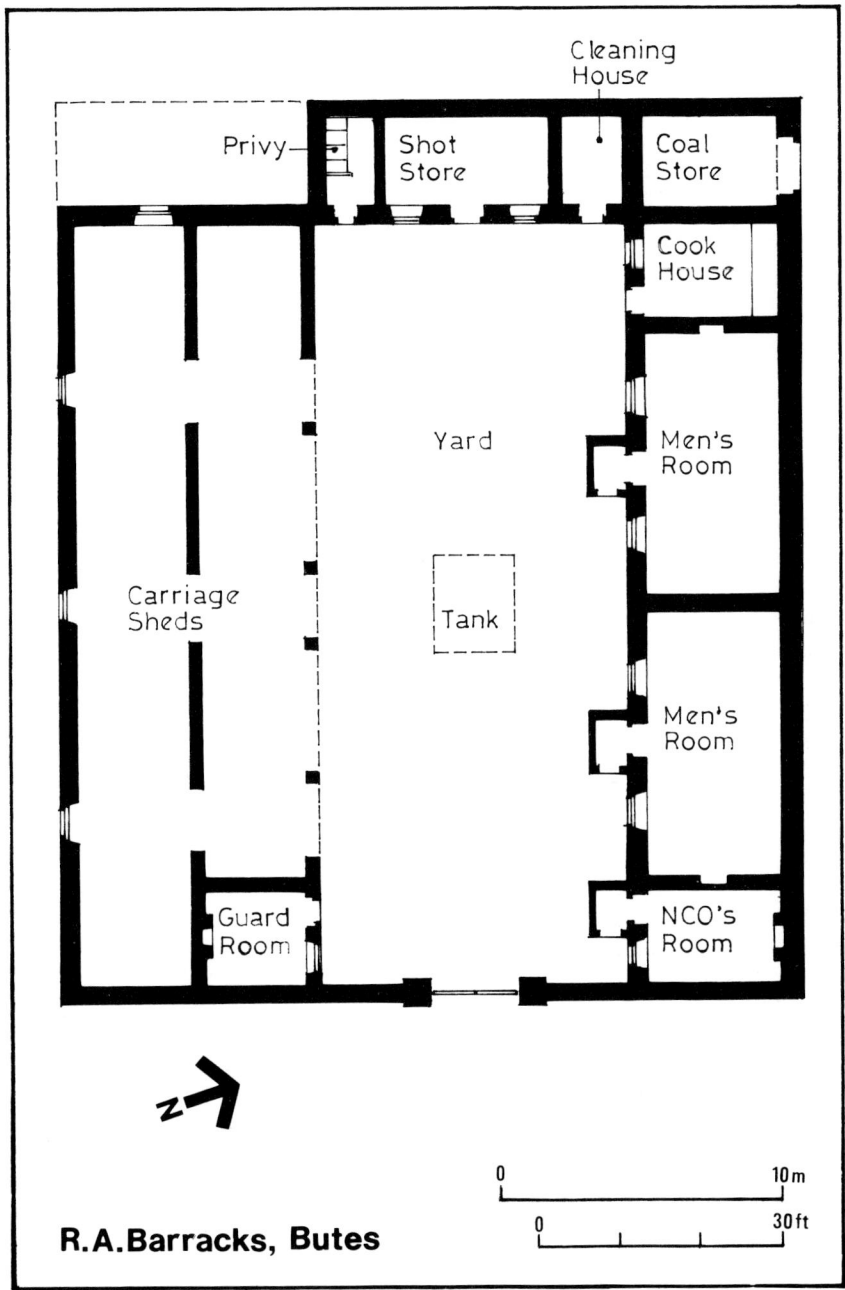

Cleaning House

Privy

Shot Store

Coal Store

Cook House

Yard

Men's Room

Carriage Sheds

Tank

Men's Room

Guard Room

NCO's Room

N

R.A. Barracks, Butes

0   10 m

0   30 ft

The Soldiers' quarters at Longis Barracks (above), built in 1801, have survived, while officers' quarters at Corblets Barracks (below) make a delightful house with part of the ruined soldiers' quarters beyond now used as a store.

The ruined Telegraph Tower to the south-west of Alderney's airport, is a prominent island landmark.

The most prominent surviving landmark from the Napoleonic Wars is Telegraph Tower, standing near the south-west cliffs. In August 1809, Sir John Doyle had approved of the recommendation that Alderney should be included in the Channel Islands telegraphic link and this led to the construction of the masonry tower on Beacon Heights, using the ingenious semaphore system devised by a Mr Mulgrave. The lower floors of the tower accommodated the officers and men employed in its service and through which vital information on the movement of French shipping could be speedily transferred to the Jersey or Guernsey squadrons when fine weather allowed.

3. THE KEY OF THE CHANNEL

Victorian pre-eminence

Alderney's Victorian fortifications are the most dominant features of the island's coastal landscape. Often described as 'castle-like' and even 'romantic', there is no denying that the ditches, drawbridges, loopholes, machicolations and other features might give this impression. As the visitor walks around the island and views them from the landward side, many do indeed have the appearance of small 'castles'. This impression is soon dispelled when seen from seaward where an experienced eye will note the formidable array of ramparts on the forts or batteries surmounting nearly every major headland or islet. This is probably most noticeable at Fort Château à L'Etoc where even the name suggests a castle. At a cursory glance from Saye or Corblets Bays, only the barrack block is clearly visible. However, from seaward, the barracks are virtually concealed; instead every available space within the main body of the fort can be imagined as bristling with guns — 23 in seven batteries was the intended armament for this work.

Perhaps the greatest attraction of Alderney's forts is their variety, although they do share common features. Wherever mountings do not exist for ordnance, provision is made for small arms fire to bear on any enemy forces that might have landed or were in the process of so doing. The numerous loopholes and musketry parapets or galleries are the most obvious features for this purpose, while the windows in many of the barrack blocks were fitted with interior, cast-iron loopholed shutters. Plans of the forts show the barrack blocks and walls to have bastions, or more precisely bastionettes, enabling the defenders to fire at the attackers along the faces should they get close. Close defence against infantry was also provided by caponiers that projected into the ditch and were loopholed for small-arms fire. Although some of the batteries are small, the size of the island must be taken into account when evaluating them as works of defence. Each was constructed with great attention to its geographical position and consequently each work differs from its neighbour.

Sir John Burgoyne's proposals of May 1852, which had so impressed Captain Jervois, were based on these principles. He emphasised the importance of Alderney's position should war break out with France as a place from which a fleet could keep a watch on the enemy's trading vessels and warships. Perhaps his most overstated argument was that, with one fifth of the defence works and one third of the garrison, Alderney would be almost as strong and be of more importance to the British Empire than Gibraltar! He went on to propose

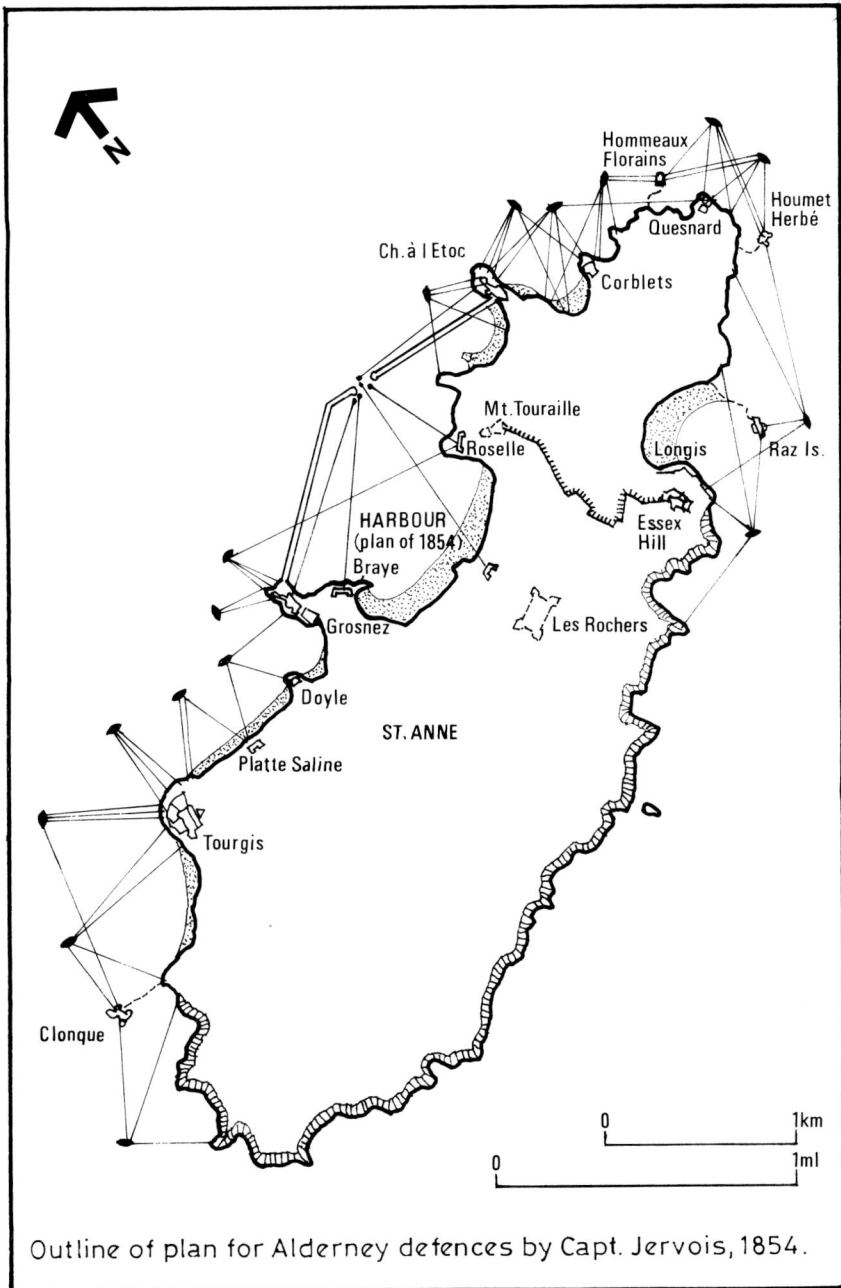

Outline of plan for Alderney defences by Capt. Jervois, 1854.

Hommeaux
Florains

Houmet
Herbé

Quesnard

Ch.à l Etoc

Corblets

Mt.Touraille

Roselle

Longis

Raz Is.

HARBOUR
(plan of 1854)

Braye

Essex
Hill

Grosnez

Les Rochers

Doyle

ST. ANNE

Platte Saline

Tourgis

Clonque

N

0   1km

0   1ml

that works defending the whole island would be preferable as it was to be expected that an attack on Alderney would comprise over 5,000 troops landing from boats at more than one place. It was estimated that up to twelve accompanying warships would both oppose the forts and batteries and cover the landings. However, no landings were anticipated within the harbour area or on the steep south and west cliffs of the island. Sir John also proposed that the disposition of the batteries would allow them to bear by direct and cross-fire, both to the front and their flanks, on any landings while being exposed as little as possible to direct fire from the warships. To oppose any landings that might occur, he proposed that the gunners, together with extra infantry, should be quartered in self-defensible blockhouses in the rear of each battery. These buildings would not only cover the gorge of the battery, but would allow musketry fire from loopholes to bear on any approaching boats.

As originally constructed, the forts and batteries had mountings for more than 220 guns, excluding mortars, of which the majority were 8-inch shell-firing guns or 68 and 32-pounder cannon; other guns included 24, 12 and 9-pounders as well as 10 and 8-inch howitzers. When the forts were constructed in the mid-1850s, they were designed to mount and receive fire from ordnance that effectively had not changed for three hundred years. The heavy gun was still a smooth-bore, muzzle-loading cannon which fired spherical solid shot or hollow explosive shell. However, mountings for the guns had become more sophisticated, making them easier to handle. The majority of the heavy guns in Alderney were on sliding traversing carriages mounted on semi-circular or circular racers and a pivot. Lighter guns were often still mounted on wheeled garrison carriages and a few of the smaller Alderney batteries had guns of this type. Most of these guns were mounted *en barbette* and fired over an earthen or stone rampart, while some fired through embrasures. Six gun positions, two in Fort Grosnez and four in Fort Albert, had overhead protection and were termed casemated; unfortunately, later British and German alterations have obliterated them.

Captain Jervois arrived in Alderney in June 1852 with a full company of Sappers and Miners and, in consultation with Sir John Burgoyne, began the task of constructing the forts. By the beginning of 1853, Fort Grosnez was nearing completion and only Rat Island Fort and Longis Lines of the new works were started. In a memorandum to the IGF in May 1854, Jervois lists all the works that were planned and eventually completed with modifications. By the end of 1855, construction of the works which can be recognised as the second phase was then nearing completion. Mount Touraille, a strategic point commanding the harbour and eastern end of the island, still had no fortified work on it. Jervois, now promoted major, had taken up another post in England but returned to Alderney when it was decided to abandon the scheme for a large redoubt for 600 men at Les Rochers. The new proposal was for a major work on Mount Touraille and this decision marked the beginning of the third and last phase of the construction programme.

Fort Albert (originally Fort Touraille), with its polygonal trace and its dual role in providing artillery defence against both land and sea attack, is unique in the history of British fortification (particularly with the addition of the German works). Of the forts in Alderney, it has had the most varied and continuing history. As the military importance of its predecessors declined, Fort Albert continued to be garrisoned, with several changes of armament, until 1929 when the Militia was disbanded and British forces were withdrawn. However, along with most of the other Victorian forts, the Second World War saw it put to new use by the Germans.

In addition to those works constructed, there were proposals for considerable additional defences. In his detailed memorandum of May 1854, Jervois outlined plans which, had they been implemented, would have made the coastline from Fort Clonque to Longis Lines an almost continuous fortified line. Sir John Burgoyne agreed with many of the recommendations and made several additional proposals of his own. Essentially these advocated the construction of extra earthen batteries in retired positions which could not be assailed by ships, and that much of the shoreline between the forts should be connected by parapet and ditch or by scarping the rock. Even as late as 1858 another Jervois memorandum recommended that Fort Touraille should be connected by a line of earthworks with Essex Hill and that those parts of the south cliffs "up which an enterprising enemy might scramble" should be scarped or have walls built. Four years earlier, there had also been proposals for wet ditches across Platte Saline and Longis foreshores, thirteen extra batteries, permanent obstructions in some of the bays and even 'catamarans' or floating mines to be fired from 'galvanic batteries' on shore. As well as these, the large redoubt at Les Rochers and a smaller one on Mannez Hill had been proposed. In the event, none of these additional defences was constructed.

The following gazetteer describes the Victorian defences of Alderney which have survived in whole or in part. The plans which accompany the descriptions of each work are based on originals in the Public Record Office, showing them in their original completed form. A key to the designations and symbols used in the plans will be found in Appendix II, on page 113.

Captain Jervois prepared several projects for Clonque Rock before the final plan was approved with the three principal batteries on the hightest points.

Fort Clonque

Fort Clonque, the most westerly of the defences, was completed in 1855 and is considered by many to be the most picturesque of the Alderney works. It stands on a small islet in the Swinge and was originally connected to Alderney by a 220 yard (200m) natural causeway which was covered at high tide. The fort was designed to mount ten guns in four batteries and to have a complement of 59 men (Barrack accommodation provided for in 1859). Nine of the guns, firing *en barbette,* were mounted in the batteries surmounting the islet's three pinnacles; the parade and both the officers' and soldiers' quarters are at the lower level. The elevated position of the three main batteries enabled the guns to enfilade Clonque and Hannaine Bays, to flank the coast and causeway and generally command the Swinge passage. A single gun, firing through an embrasure, was set in the centre of the musketry parapet on the north-east face. The scarped wall of this face is flanked both by the 'bomb-proof kitchen' and 'guard house', both acting as caponiers. Overlooking Hannaine Bay, the south-east wall is loopholed for musketry as is the west face of the latrines which are below the soldiers' quarters. The fort is separated from the causeway by a dry ditch with a drawbridge.

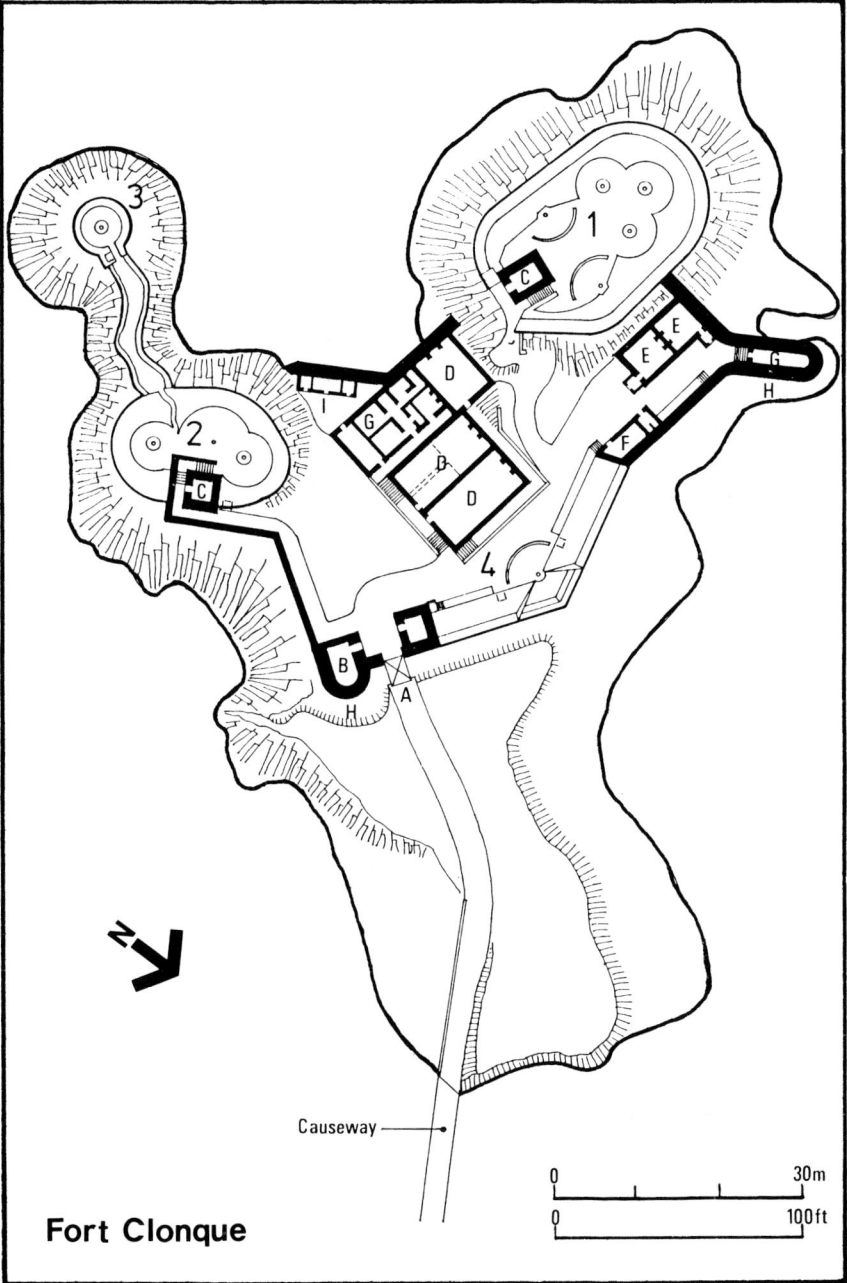

3

1

2

C

D

D

D

D

E
E

F

G
H

B
H

A

4

I

G

N

Causeway

0		30m
0		100 ft

Fort Clonque

49

A caponier protects the west face of Battery No. 1 at Fort Tourgis.

Fort Tourgis

Completed in 1855, Fort Tourgis is the second largest of the Alderney forts and was designed to mount 33 guns in five batteries and have a complement of 346 men. Its position, at the north-west point of the island on a low headland known as Rocque Tourgie, was such that its guns would cover both Clonque and Platte Saline Bays. The three main batteries all have pivot and racer mountings for guns firing *en barbette* over earthen ramparts with masonry revetments. Each battery has its own magazine, shell store and fuze-fixing room.

The masonry scarps of Nos. 1 and 2 batteries, each having eight guns, have bastion-like traces and are flanked by musketry caponiers in shallow ditches at the salient angles.

Lying between these batteries but set back and slightly uphill, is No. 3 battery; four guns fired to the front while three fired to each flank thus commanding the lower batteries should they be overrun. Platforms for four mortars were also sited here. Two other guns, having an arc of fire of about 270 degrees, were mounted at the salient angles in two small bastions. These two bastions are joined by an earthen musketry parapet which runs in front of and below the main rampart with the masonry scarp joining that of the Nos. 1 and 2 batteries on either side. It appears that provision was made here for frontal musketry fire with the western flank of No. 1 battery being an extended musketry parapet, while the eastern flank of No. 2 battery consists of a loopholed wall. Access from No. 3 battery to the lower batteries was afforded by means of two drawbridges across a ditch.

50

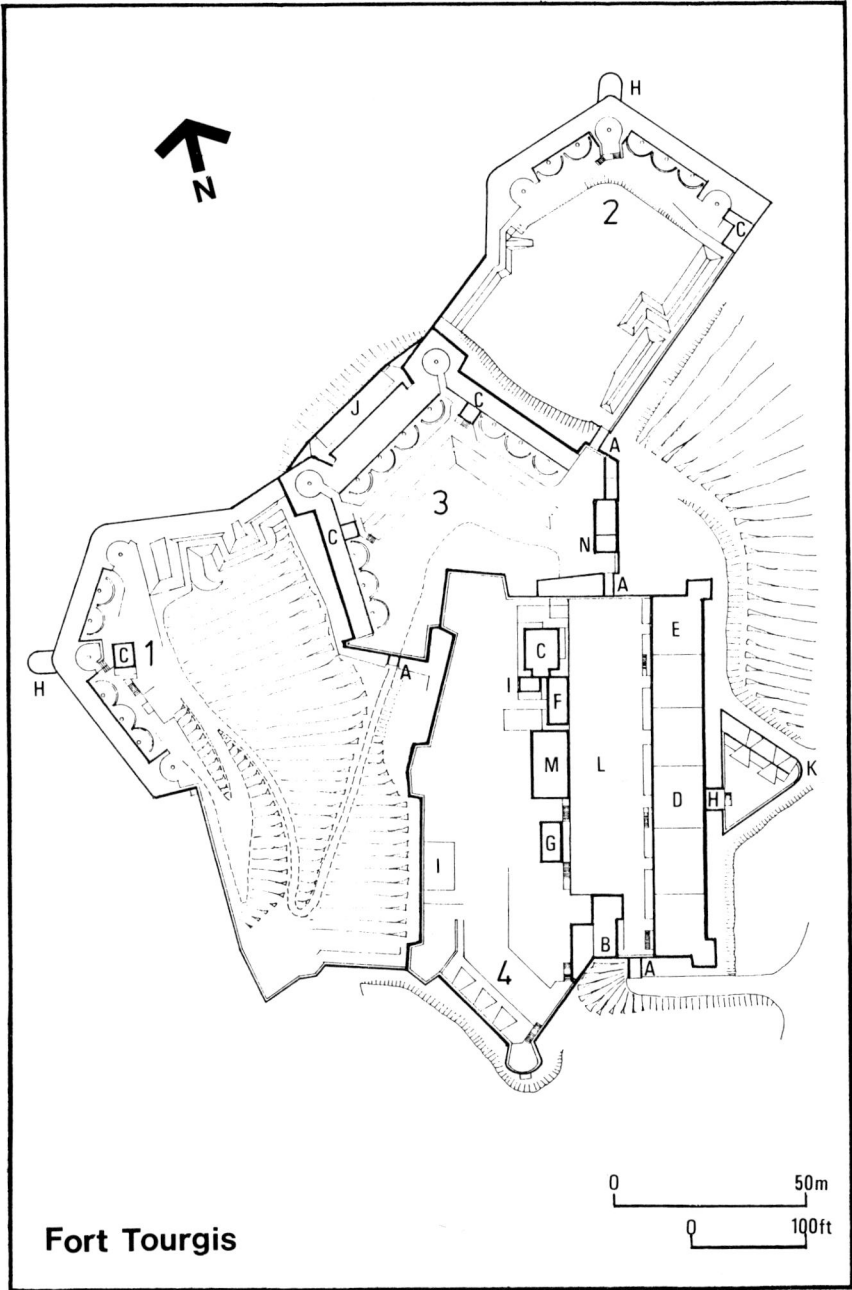

N

H

2

C

J

C

3

C

A

N

A

E

C

I

F

H

1

M

L

K

D

H

I

G

I

B

A

4

0   50m

0   100ft

Fort Tourgis

Fort Tourgis from the air, showing the citadel and outlying batteries (Aerofilms).

The east wall of the barracks at Fort Tourgis is linked to the redan by a short caponier.

Behind and uphill is the citadel containing the barrack block. Access to it is gained from the central battery by a third drawbridge. The citadel is regular in plan with a salient on the southern face to allow a battery of three guns, mounted on garrison standing carriages and firing through arched embrasures, to enfilade the beach at Clonque Bay; the other face of this salient is loopholed and flanks the entrance to the fort. The eastern wall of the barrack block is protected by a redan with two guns firing towards Platte Saline and a loopholed wall facing inland; access to the redan is via a caponier which is also loopholed and flanks the ditch along the eastern wall of the barracks. Small bastionettes, at each corner of the citadel, flank the walls which are loopholed on all sides; in addition the east windows of the barrack block were fitted with interior cast-iron loopholed shutters.

German defences have been built on the west face of Doyle's Battery to enfilade Platte Saline.

Platte Saline Battery

In 1854 plans for a reserve battery of three guns situated to the north of Fort Tourgis barracks were shelved when it was decided to build a battery in the centre of Platte Saline Bay. As this beach offered an excellent landing site for an enemy force, it was considered more expedient to build a detached battery adjacent to the earlier open battery to the west. In design it is the simplest of the Alderney works, having five guns *en barbette* facing north with a guard room only. At either end of the battery, the artillery store and fuze-fixing room are loopholed as is the south-facing gorge wall. The entrance is to the west of the loopholed guard room which is centrally set at an angle of 45 degrees in the gorge wall so that small arms fire would flank the rear of the battery.

Doyle's Battery

Situated about 435 yards (400m) to the east of Platte Saline Battery, Doyle's Battery is built on a rocky headland and commands both the eastern end of Platte Saline and Crabby Bay. Completed in 1854, it is the smallest of Alderney's Victorian works being designed for four guns with quarters for a complement of 22 men. Three of the guns, mounted *en barbette* but close together, fired to seaward and both flanks. The fourth gun, mounted on a garrison standing carriage, fired westward through an embrasure towards Platte Saline beach. The rear wall of the battery is irregular in shape, but is bastioned and contains numerous musketry loopholes.

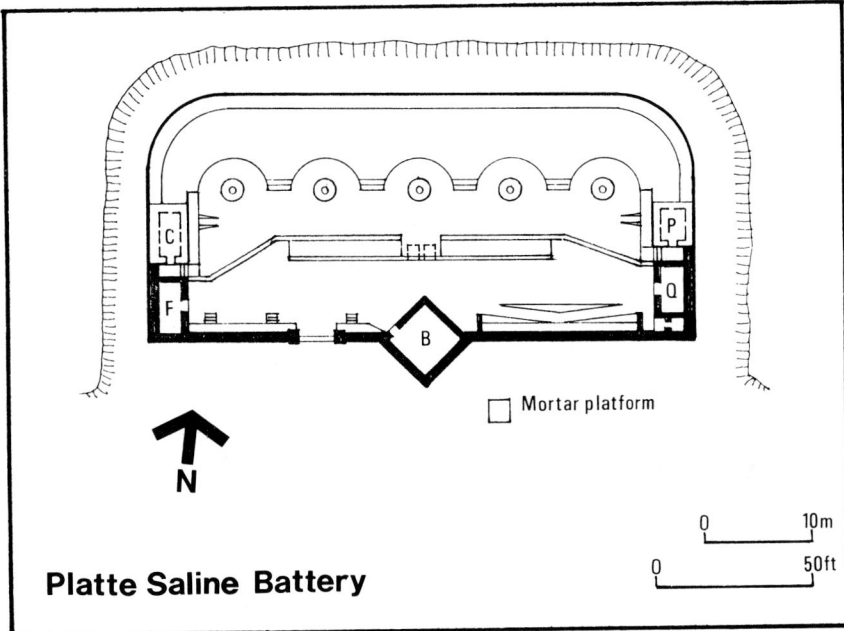

Platte Saline Battery

Mortar platform

0   10m

0   50ft

N

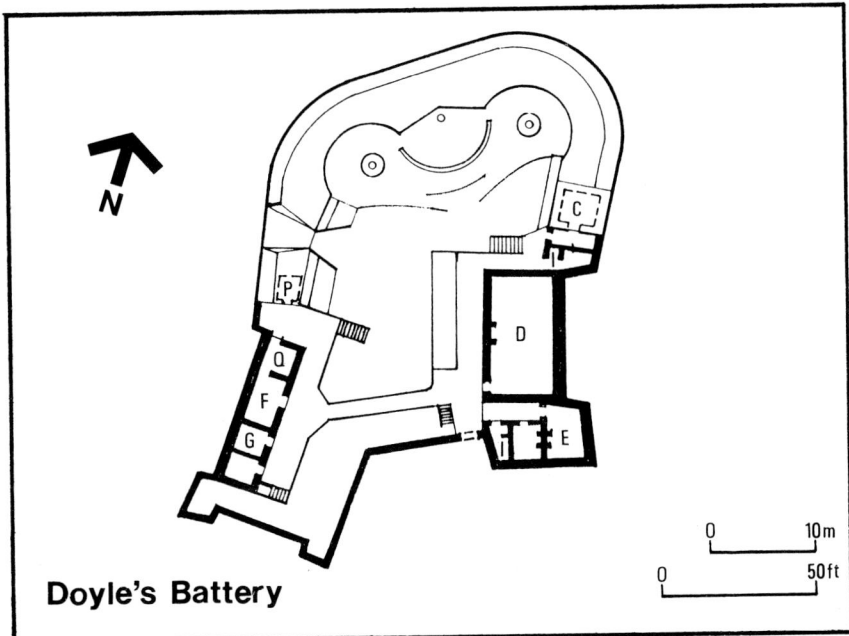

Doyle's Battery

N

0   10m

0   50ft

The impressive west face of Fort Grosnez, seen from Doyle's Battery, extends seawards to the casemated tower.

Fort Grosnez

Constructed between 1850 and 1853, Fort Grosnez was the first fort to be completed. It was designed with bomb-proof barracks for three officers and 112 men. Of the larger forts, it was the only one designed to have an all-round field of fire for its 28 heavy guns in seven batteries; its main purpose was to protect the breakwater and harbour from both sea and land attack.

The fort differs from the others in Alderney in that it is constructed entirely of dressed blocks of coursed, red sandstone, while the casemated tower built at its northern end to flank the breakwater is contructed entirely of grey ashlar granite masonry.

Perhaps the most interesting feature of Fort Grosnez is its defence against land attack. On the landward side is a glacis, originally stone covered on its lower section, having masonry supporting walls. Commanding the glacis is a high cavalier with the guns of No. 1 battery firing through embrasures, positioned to sweep the glacis and beyond; two 8-inch howitzers were also mounted for land defence. The high, south-facing rampart is designed to protect the inside of the fort from plunging fire from enemy artillery that might be established on the island. The cavalier is separated from the glacis by a revetted dry ditch which is flanked by a central musketry caponier; the caponier is itself flanked by a loopholed scarp gallery. Entry to the fort was effected by means of a rolling bridge in the ditch. Under the cavalier, adjacent to the entrance tunnel, scarp gallery and a guard house/caponier, is No. 1 magazine.

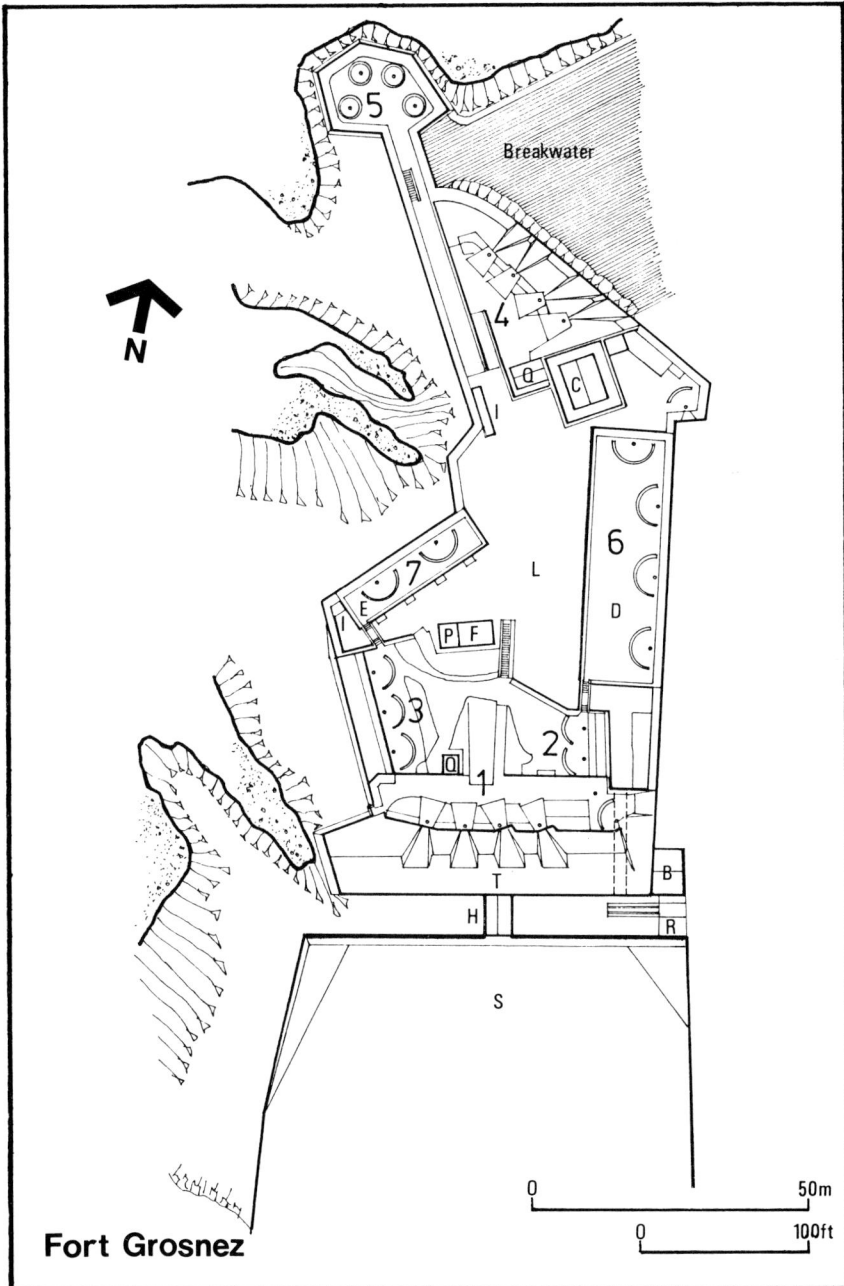

Breakwater

N

5

4

O

C

6

L

D

7

E

P F

3

2

1

O

T

B

H

R

S

Fort Grosnez

0   50m

0   100ft

The original Victorian casemate embrasures at Fort Grosnez tower have been infilled and replaced by German 10.5 cm and 4.7 cm positions.

Batteries Nos. 2, 3, 6, and 7 are reached from the parade by means of a gun ramp which continues up to No. 1 battery on the cavalier. Batteries Nos. 6 and 7 are situated on top of the bomb-proof soldiers' and officers' quarters respectively.

The northernmost granite tower contained two guns in casemates flanking the seaward side of the breakwater; above, at the 32 foot (9.75m) level, four guns were mounted *en barbette* firing towards the front and flanks. However, the only remaining evidence of these mountings is the blocked up casemate embrasures as the Germans converted the tower into a reinforced concrete strongpoint.

In between and below the various batteries, and along both walls of the fort, numerous loopholes provided for small arms fire to bear both into the harbour and Crabby Bay.

Braye Battery

Stretching from the landward end of Douglas Quay to the site of the present harbour office, Braye Battery was designed to mount nine guns firing *en barbette* to the north-east to cover the harbour roads and entrance. The guns were mounted in three staggered pairs and a trio, each group being separated by an earthern traverse as protection against enfilade from seaward. Within the battery perimeter were an artillery store, the Royal Engineers' office and a guard room. With the exception of the RE office (now known as Harbour House) and the guard room, all that remains of this battery today are short sections of parapet wall and a few lumps of granite cut to fit a racer mounting and pivot. The battery was not self-defensible, being exposed to assault only on the successful reduction of Fort Grosnez.

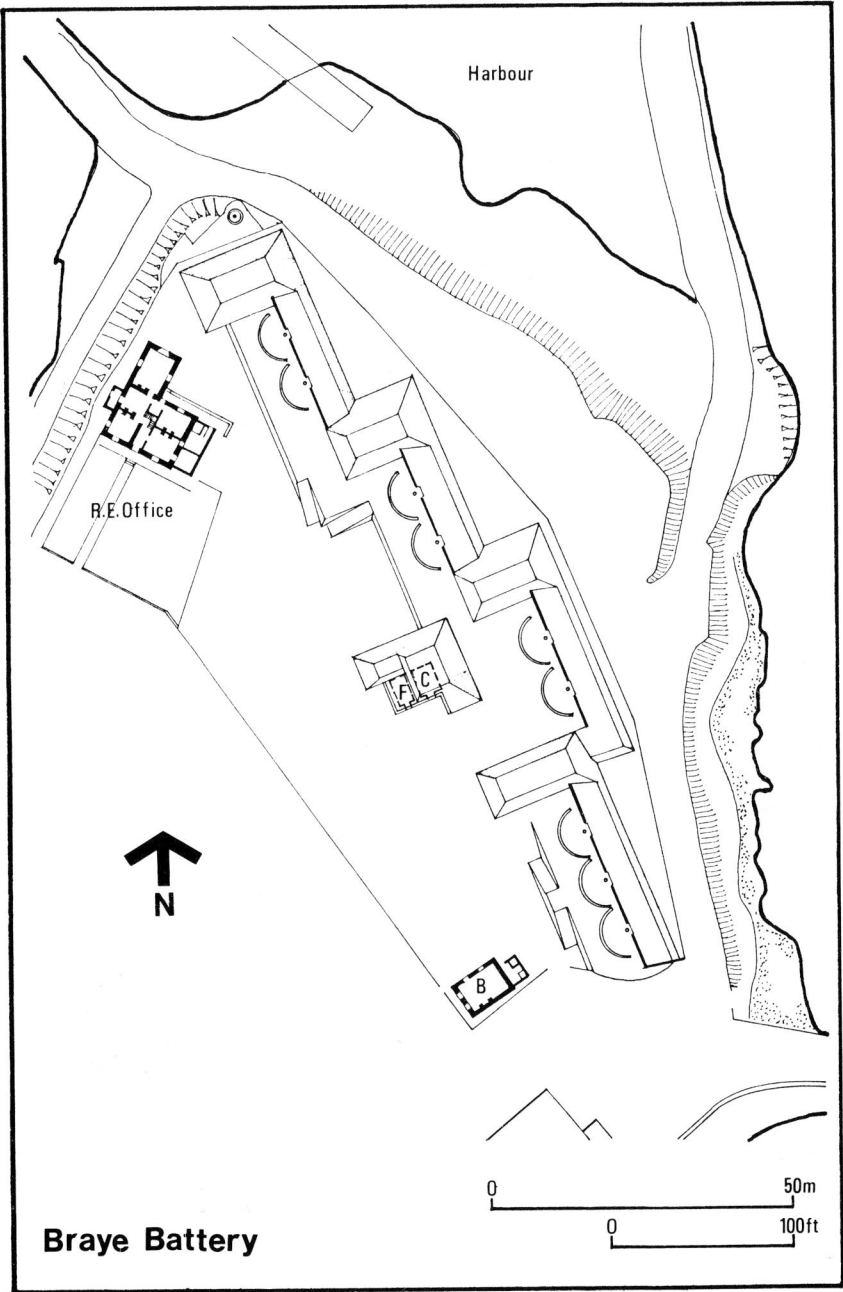

Harbour

R.E.Office

F C

B

N

0   50m

0   100ft

Braye Battery

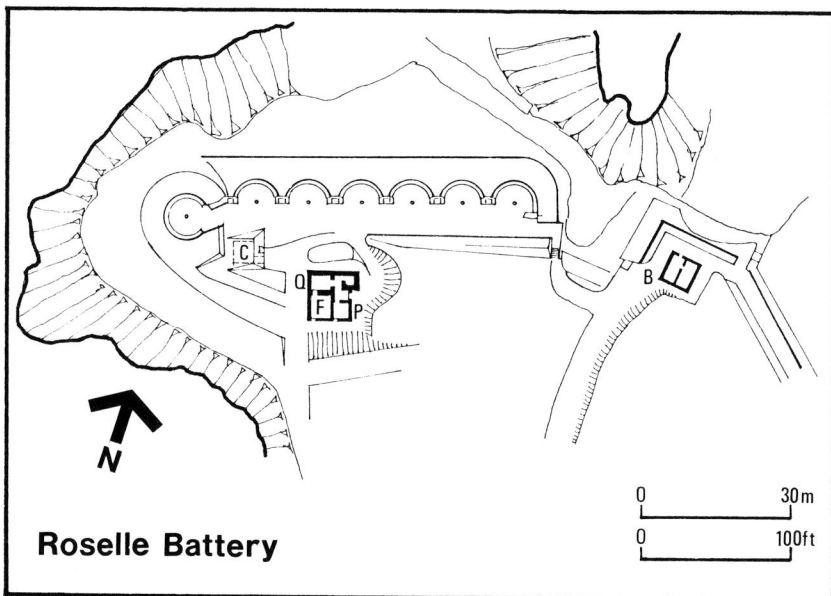

Roselle Battery

Roselle Battery

Roselle Battery, originally the site of an earlier battery, was re-designed for seven guns to protect the entrance to the harbour. Within the battery perimeter was a guardhouse and magazine. Access from Fort Albert was by both road and a protected walk way via a sally port in the north-west ditch.

The battery was completed by 1854 before Fort Albert, the island's major work, was conceived. At this time the eastern arm of the breakwater was planned to extend westwards from Bibette Head; Roselle Battery would then have provided the major defence for the harbour entrance. However, with the plan to increase the size of the harbour and to build Fort Albert in 1856, its original purpose was superceded. When the decision was taken to abandon the harbour works in 1872 and to restrict the harbour to its present size, it ensured that the battery would continue to play a major role in defending the harbour entrance. In 1899, after having been disarmed, two 12-pounder quick-firing guns with crew shelter under and two associated defence electric lights were installed to cover the harbour entrance and examination anchorage at the same time as the two 6-inch breech-loading guns at Fort Albert. While the electric light directing post remains at the eastern end of the modified battery, as do the small artillery store and magazine at the rear, only one of the 12-pounder positions is partially visible under the German additions.

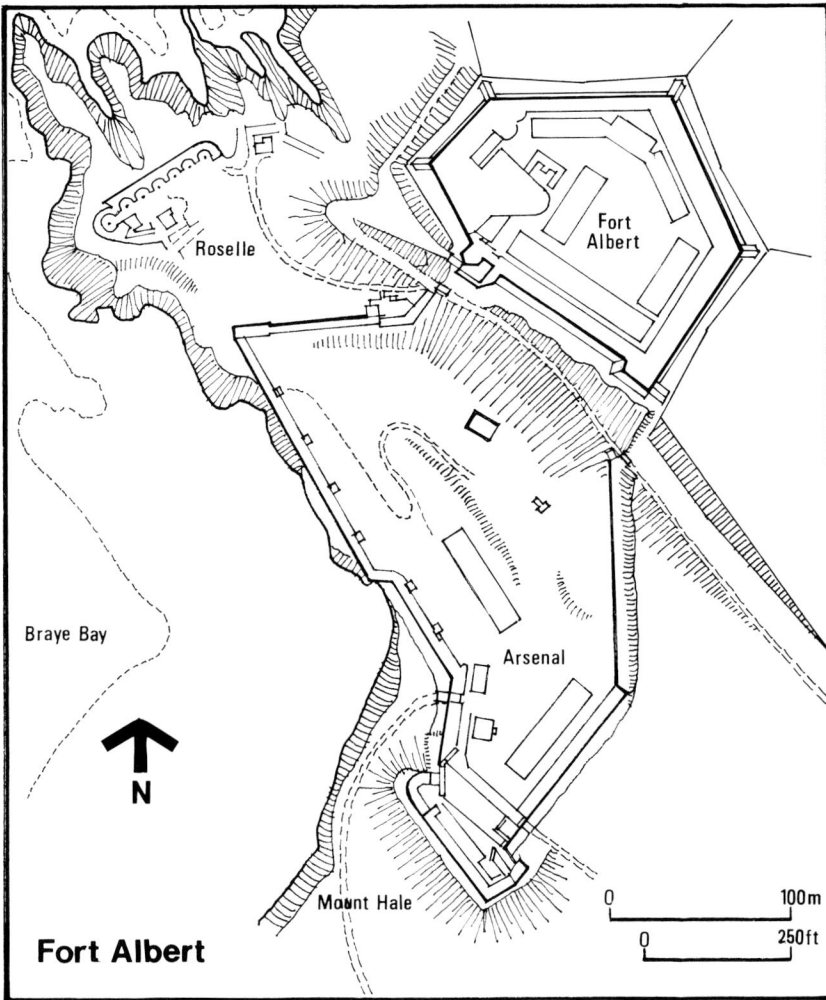

Fort Albert

Roselle

Braye Bay

N

Fort Albert

Arsenal

Mount Hale

| 0 | 100 m |
| 0 | 250 ft |

Fort Albert

Fort Touraille, later to be re-named Fort Albert following the death of the Prince Consort, was constructed between 1856 and 1859 and was the last of the forts to be built. The design shows many features that set it apart from its predecessors on the island with its low profile, polygonal trace, extensive glacis, deep ditch flanked by musketry caponiers, and ramparts designed to mount as many guns as possible. The original plan shows it to have mountings for 35 guns on the ramparts and eight more on the cavalier.

The massive ramparts of Fort Albert command the approach road.

The heaviest fire from Nos. 2, 3 and 4 batteries would enfilade Saye, Corblets and Longis Bays, while that from No. 1 battery and the cavalier would flank the harbour. Only the south-west rampart mounted no guns; here a musketry parapet overlooks the Arsenal and Store Establishment, Mount Hale Battery and the approaches to the fort's entrance.

With the installation of two 6-inch BL guns at the turn of the century, a major alteration to the north-west corner of the fort was carried out. Not even the works associated with the German naval battery during the Second World War had as much impact on the fort's appearance.

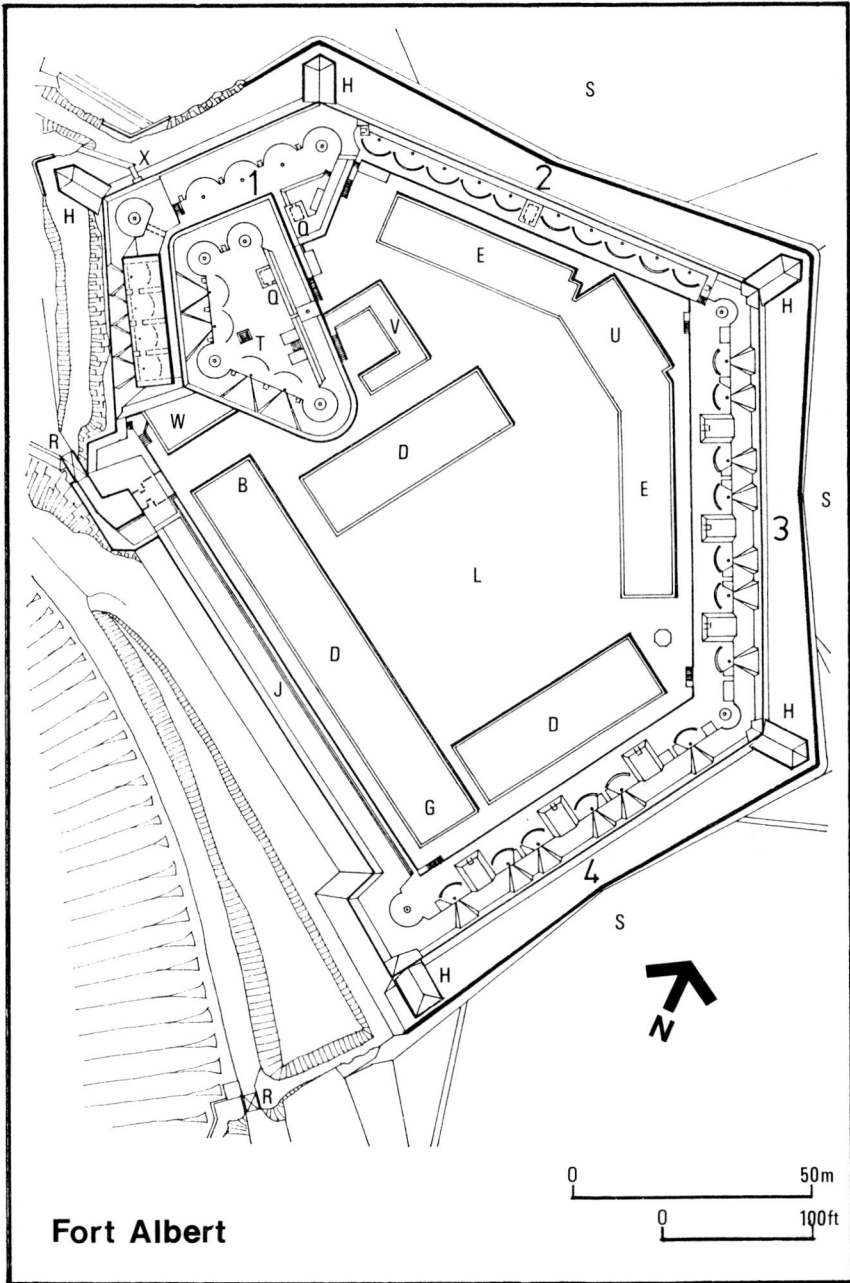

Fort Albert

H

S

X

·1

H

Q

2

E

H

O

Q

V

U

T

E

W

R

D

B

E

3

S

L

J

D

D

H

G

D

4

H

S

R

N

0   50m

0   100ft

Looking east along the ditch and terreplein of Battery No. 2 at Fort Albert, British concrete pillboxes of the First World War period and a German 17 cm gun emplacement have been superimposed on the original Victorian gun positions.

In constructing the standard reinforced concrete emplacements for the twin 6-inch gun battery and magazine, the platforms for the eight guns on the cavalier, the five guns of No. 1 battery and the four west-facing casemated guns were removed. The cavalier was also reduced in height by some 12 feet (3.6m), the loopholed musketry parapet and gallery below No. 1 battery were blocked up and the rampart was built up with earth and a sand layer. This gave the 6-inch guns, now the fort's only armament, an all-round field of fire. Beneath the old No. 1 battery is the remains of a scarp gallery with access to both No. 5 caponier and the blocked up sally port into the ditch.

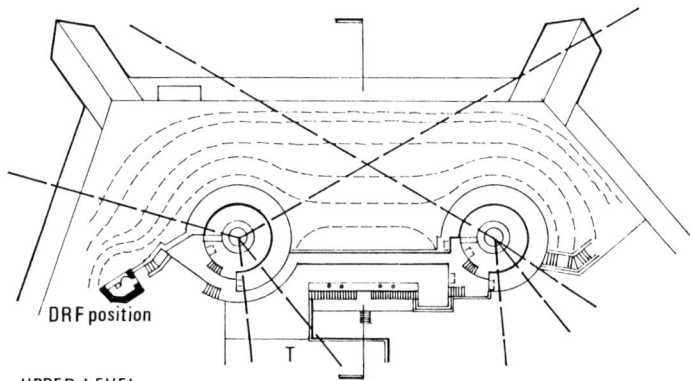

DRF position

UPPER LEVEL

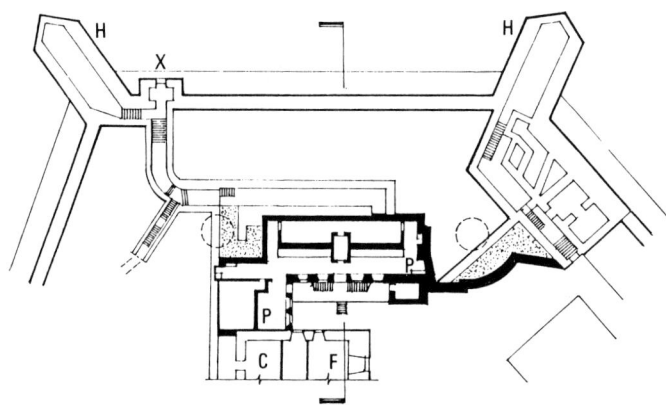

H   X   H

P

P

C   F

LOWER LEVEL

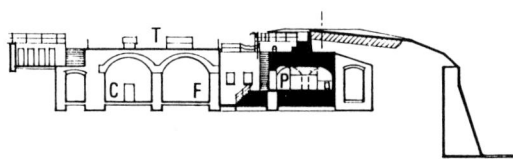

T

C   F

SECTION

6-in B.L. Battery

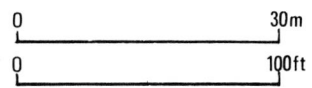

0   30m

0   100ft

Fort Albert, seen from the air, before the demolition of the barracks (Aerofilms).

From Mount Hale Battery, looking north to Roselle Point, a fine view can be gained of the musketry parapet and loopholed gallery of the Arsenal.

Beneath the ramparts of Nos. 3 and 4 batteries are fine examples of continuous, brick-vaulted scarp galleries with associated magazines, shafts for hoisting ammunition, storage vaults, caponier flanking galleries and stairways to the caponiers. The counterfort arches beneath both No. 2 battery and the musketry parapet overlooking the Arsenal complex, provided space for supporting services and amenities for the garrison. Barrack accommodation consisted of single storey, brick-vaulted, flat-roofed buildings that housed some 424 officers and men.

The approach to the fort was by a track from Whitegates across three rolling bridges; two as the track passed through the outer defensive walls of the Arsenal and the third across the ditch at the entrance to the fort.

Mount Hale Battery

Constructed in 1858 on a small hill from which it took its name to the south-west of Fort Albert, Mount Hale Battery was part of the Arsenal complex and served three purposes. First, its occupation prevented the hill from falling into enemy hands or leaving an area of dead ground to the south; secondly, its fire would flank the walls of the Arsenal and thirdly, its wide terreplein would allow mortars to enfilade Braye beach should an enemy reach the shore. There is only one gun mounting in the battery which fired northwards enfilading the masonry scarp of the Arsenal's west face; on the south side a parapet and loopholed walls gave protection from a land attack. The ditch outside the battery joined with that formerly protecting the Arsenal.

67

Commanded by Fort Albert, with the elevated Mount Hale Battery placed to enfilade Braye beach, the principal Store Establishment and Arsenal buildings were also enclosed within a defensive perimeter wall.

The Arsenal and Store Establishment

The Arsenal and Store Establishment, together with Mount Hale Battery, can be regarded as outworks of Fort Albert. The complex occupies the low ground to the east of Braye Bay and is commanded by the musketry parapet on the massive, battered, west wall of Fort Albert. Enclosing the whole complex to the south-east is a wall, loopholed in part, with a ditch; to the north, a fine brick-vaulted, loopholed musketry gallery enfilades the entire outwork. The upper end of this gallery opens onto a small battery with magazine and guardhouse. From here two guns, on garrison carriages and firing through embrasures, could sweep the slopes below. Overlooking the beach are a series of adjacent musketry parapets.

The buildings within the Arsenal formed the permanent Ordnance establishment with the Ordnance Storekeeper's house and office, the Commissariat, barrack and general stores, coal store, gunsheds for mobile field artillery, shot stores and the small-arms magazine. A ball court (now the island's squash court) and the principal well, which supplied Fort Albert, also lie within the walls of the Arsenal.

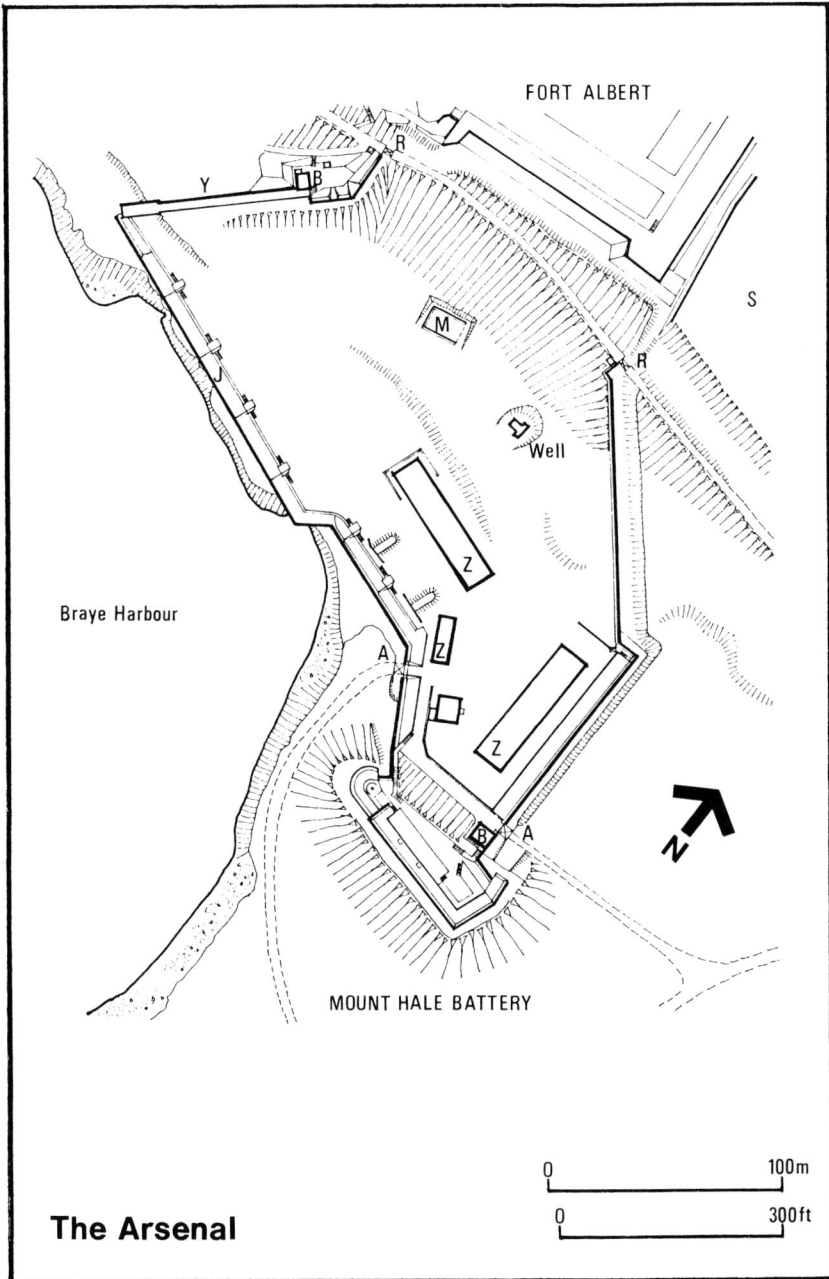

FORT ALBERT

Y

B

R

M

S

R

J

Well

Z

Braye Harbour

A

Z

Z

Z

B

A

N

MOUNT HALE BATTERY

| 0 | | 100 m |
| 0 | | 300 ft |

The Arsenal

Viewed from the sea, Fort Chateau à l'Etoc exhibits the true offensive face of Alderney's chain of forts and batteries.

Fort Chateau à L'Etoc

Completed in 1855, the fort is situated at the most northerly point of the island on the narrow headland separating Saye and Corblets Bays. Because of its excellent flanking position, it was designed to mount 23 guns in seven batteries and have barrack accommodation for 128 officers and men.

Due to the shape of the headland, it is the most amorphous of the Alderney forts and has little wasted space. Only by inspecting the plan of the fort can its function be fully realised. The chevron-shaped three-storey barrack block, with its corner bastionettes, roof parapet, ditch and cast-iron loopholed window shutters, was obviously designed to cover with small-arms fire any possible landing in the adjacent bays. The ends of the barracks are protected by earthern traverses beneath which are the two principal magazines.

The seven batteries take up all of the remaining space apart from a few sections of linking wall which are loopholed. In order that extra fire could be brought to bear on either flank, the six guns of No. 1 battery are raised on a cavalier; this also acts as a further protection for the barracks. At the northern tip, the elevated Hermitage Battery originally mounted two guns and is reached by climbing steps to a level some 15 feet (4.5m) above the adjoining batteries.

As built, the fort was a much modified version of the earlier plans designed to suit the Admiralty's final decision to commence the eastern breakwater for the enlarged harbour from Chateau à L'Etoc.

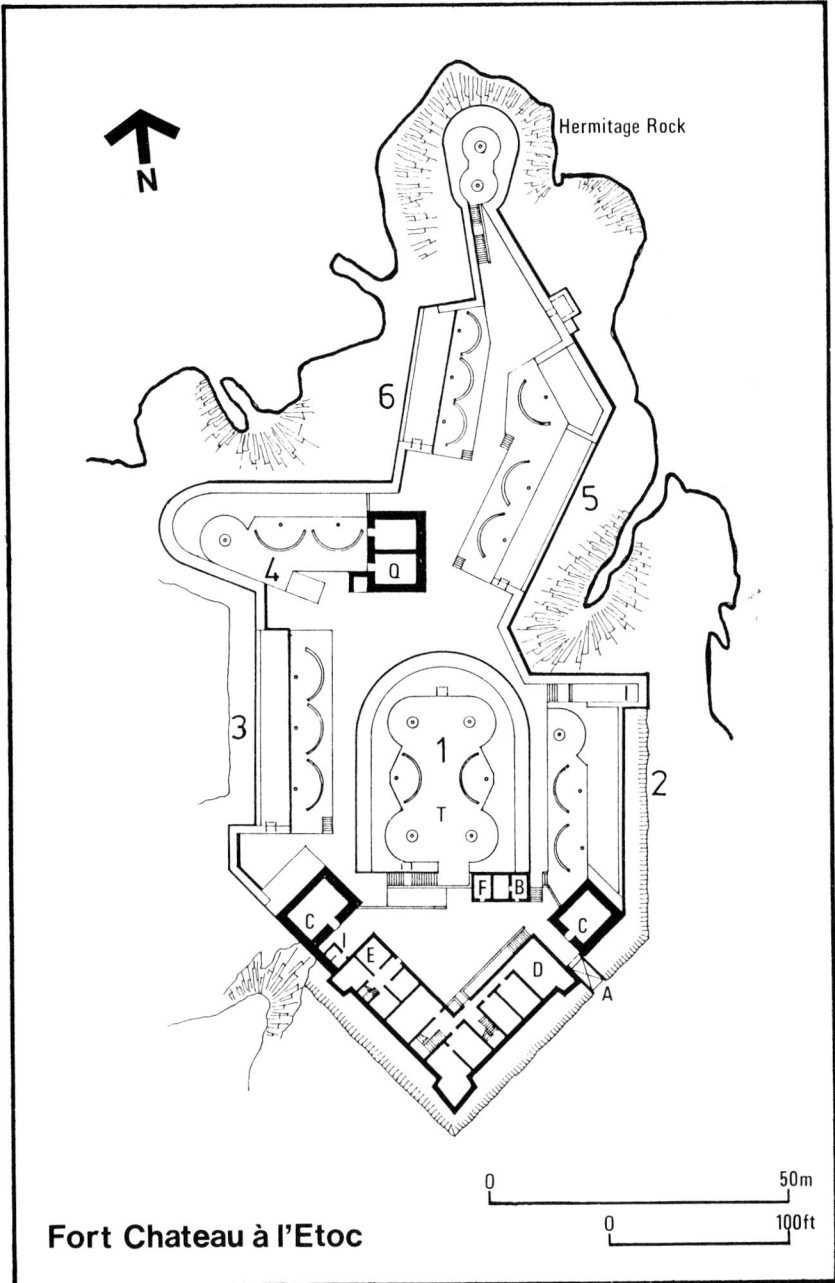

N

Hermitage Rock

6

5

4   Q

3   1   2
              T

         F B

     C   C
   E
         D   A

0   50m

0   100ft

Fort Chateau à l'Etoc

Fort Corblets, in spite of its conversion to a dwelling, retains the principal features of the original design.

Fort Corblets

Situated on the headland between Corblets and Vaux Trembliers Bays, Fort Corblets had mountings for thirteen guns in four batteries and accommodation for 59 officers and men when completed in 1855. Nos. 1, 2 and 3 batteries were situated on rounded salients and were designed to fire to seaward and both flanks. The fire from the three guns, on garrison carriages, of No. 4 battery was directed eastwards to cover any enemy assault that might succeed in reaching the shore. Two small bastions flank the gorge and the east and west faces of the fort, while small-arms fire from the soldiers' quarters would cover Corblets Bay. A loopholed machicolation is positioned over the entrance to the fort, which formerly had a drawbridge across a rock-cut ditch.

Fort Les Hommeaux Florains

This fort for 67 officers and men was constructed on a small island at the north-eastern tip of Alderney and, although begun in 1854, was not completed until 1859 due to the difficulties imposed by its remote position; it was subsequently abandoned just thirty years later.

Three guns *en barbette* covered the seaward approaches while two guns firing through arched embrasures flanked the bays on either side. The magazine and part of the soldiers' quarters were constructed in casemates beneath the seaward-facing ramparts, while the main barrack accommodation was at the rear. The walls and gorge were loopholed and flanked by two small bastions. The fort was originally reached by a tidal causeway, the last section comprising a short trestle bridge giving access to a drawbridge.

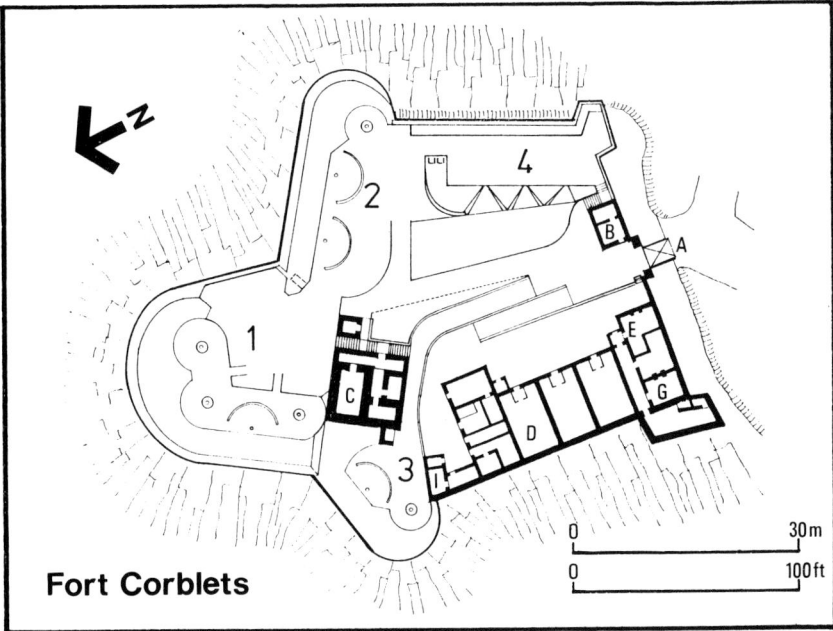

Fort Corblets

0   30m
0   100ft

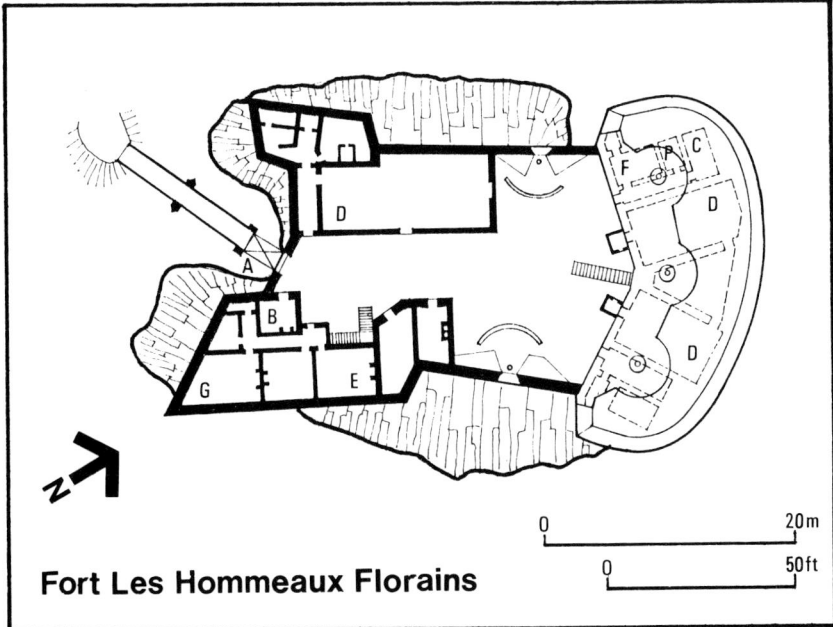

Fort Les Hommeaux Florains

0   20m
0   50ft

One of three German Flak positions is mounted on the battery at Fort Quesnard with its detached barracks.

Fort Quesnard

Completed in 1855, Fort Quesnard lies on the south-east side of Cats Bay and is of unusual design. The fort's seven guns were mounted *en barbette* in a detached semi-circular battery. As this left no room for small-arms fire to flank the vulnerable Cats Bay to the north-west, a small loopholed scarp gallery was constructed beneath the main ramparts to remedy this.

Designed for a complement of 55 officers and men, the barrack block was isolated from the battery by a ditch and drawbridge. Flanking this ditch was a small open musketry caponier in the centre of the gorge wall of the battery. The two storey barrack block is self-defensible with a rock-cut ditch and bastionettes at each corner; this allowed for musketry fire to flank the walls both in the ditch and at ground level. Access to the barracks was by means of a drawbridge.

Fort Houmet Herbé

Vying with Fort Clonque as the most picturesque of the Alderney forts, Fort Houmet Herbé is situated on a small island which is cut off at high tide. Completed in 1854 and designed for a complement of 61 men, it is medieval in appearance with its four low rounded towers at each corner; these towers mounted five guns *en barbette,* three having an all-round field of fire. It was the unlikelihood of an attack by infantry from the landward side that allowed the designer to dispense with the corner bastionettes usually seen in the Alderney forts. This allowed two of the guns to cover both the original tidal causeway and the beaches of St. Esquere and Grounard Bays.

74

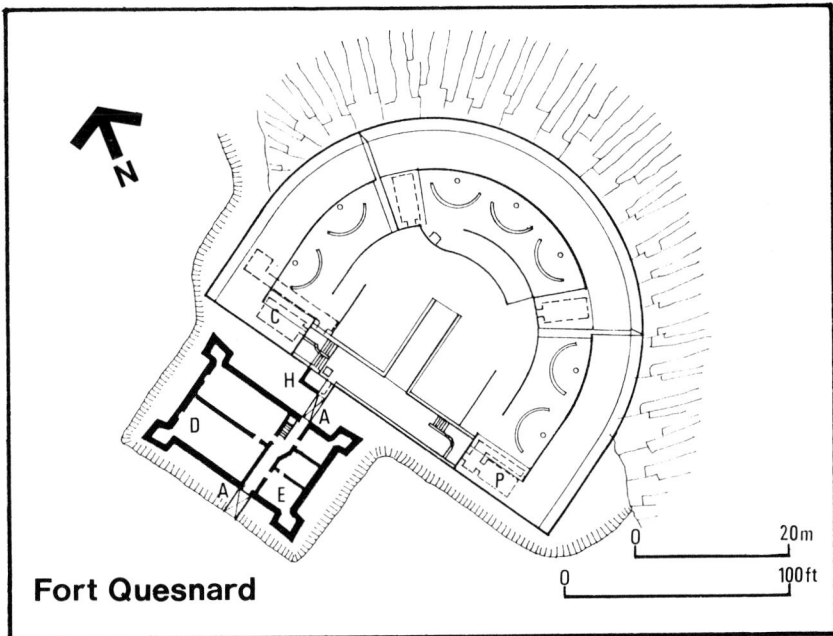

Fort Quesnard

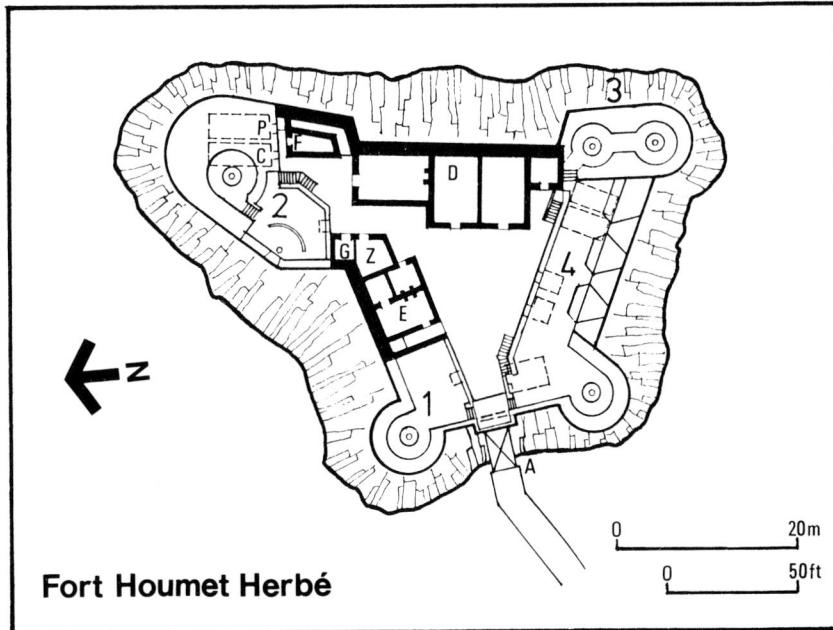

Fort Houmet Herbé

75

The single barbette gun positions on their round corner towers give Fort Houmet Herbé its distinctive appearance.

A single gun firing through an embrasure and a second *en barbette* covered St Esquere Bay to the north, while three other guns on garrison carriages, firing through embrasures in an earthen rampart into Grounard Bay to the south, completed its armament.

The walls between the corner towers are loopholed for musketry and the entrance and drawbridge were protected by a machicolation. The fort's ten guns were manned by a complement of ten officers and 51 men housed in the compact barrack rooms.

Fort Ile de Raz

Known to the Victorians as Rat Island Fort it was, together with Longis Lines, completed in 1855 during the second construction phase. Reached by a tidal causeway, the fort mounted ten guns in two batteries firing to seaward and into Longis Bay. Behind, and 15 feet (4.5m) below the rampart level, is a well-protected barracks for two officers and 64 men; the magazine and fuze-fixing room are similarly protected.

The north-east facing scarp of the battery and the entrance are flanked by a bomb-proof guard room or caponier, while a smaller second caponier, doubling as the lock-up, flanks the south-east facing scarp. The elongated barrack block is flanked by a shallow, central bastion comprising the officers' quarters and the walls are loopholed. Access to the fort was by drawbridge across a shallow ditch.

76

The barrack block of Fort Ile de Raz, seen from the elevated battery with, in the distance, a section of the German anti-tank wall lining Longis Bay.

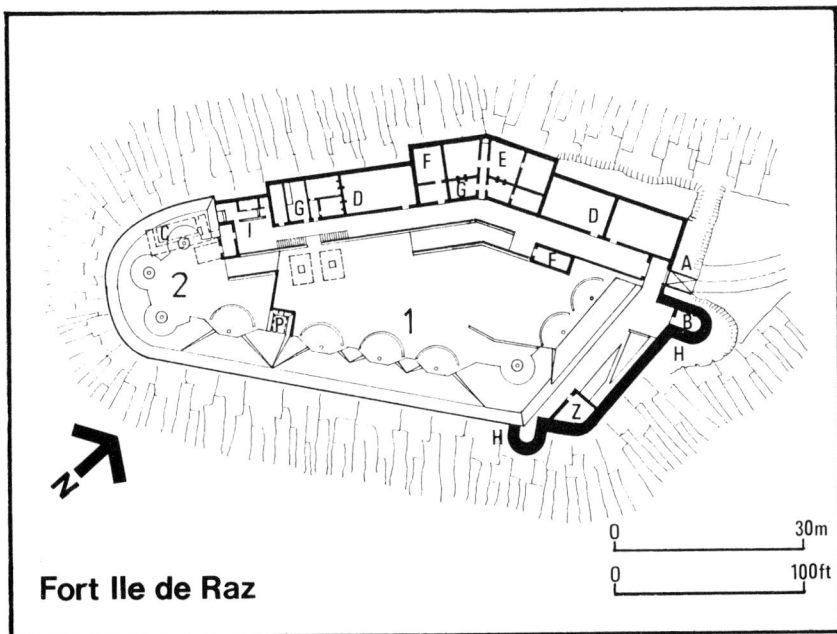

Fort Ile de Raz

0   30m

0   100ft

The masonry scarp wall to Longis Lines extends from the Frying Pan Battery (left), following an irregular trace along the western side of the bay.

Longis Lines

Longis Lines lie to the east of and below Essex Barracks and were sited on an earlier battery which was part of the defences during the Napoleonic Wars. The lines, together with Rat Island Fort, were sited to effectively seal the entrance to Longis Bay.

The design was for fourteen guns to fire *en barbette* over an earthen rampart; the 20 feet (6m) high masonry scarp simply follows the coastline in a north/south direction. The southernmost mounting, sited on a salient and known as Frying Pan Battery, had an arc of fire that would enable it to cover any landing to the south-west. North of the lines, the breastwork of the earlier battery may still be seen with behind it the old barracks used by the Victorians to accommodate three officers and twenty men.

West of the battery entrance, the large, well-protected magazine which served the lines is probably the finest and best preserved on the island. It was originally intended to connect Longis Lines with Essex Barracks in a similar fashion to Fort Albert and the Arsenal complex. If completed it would have made the whole position defensible against infantry, but this work was never carried out.

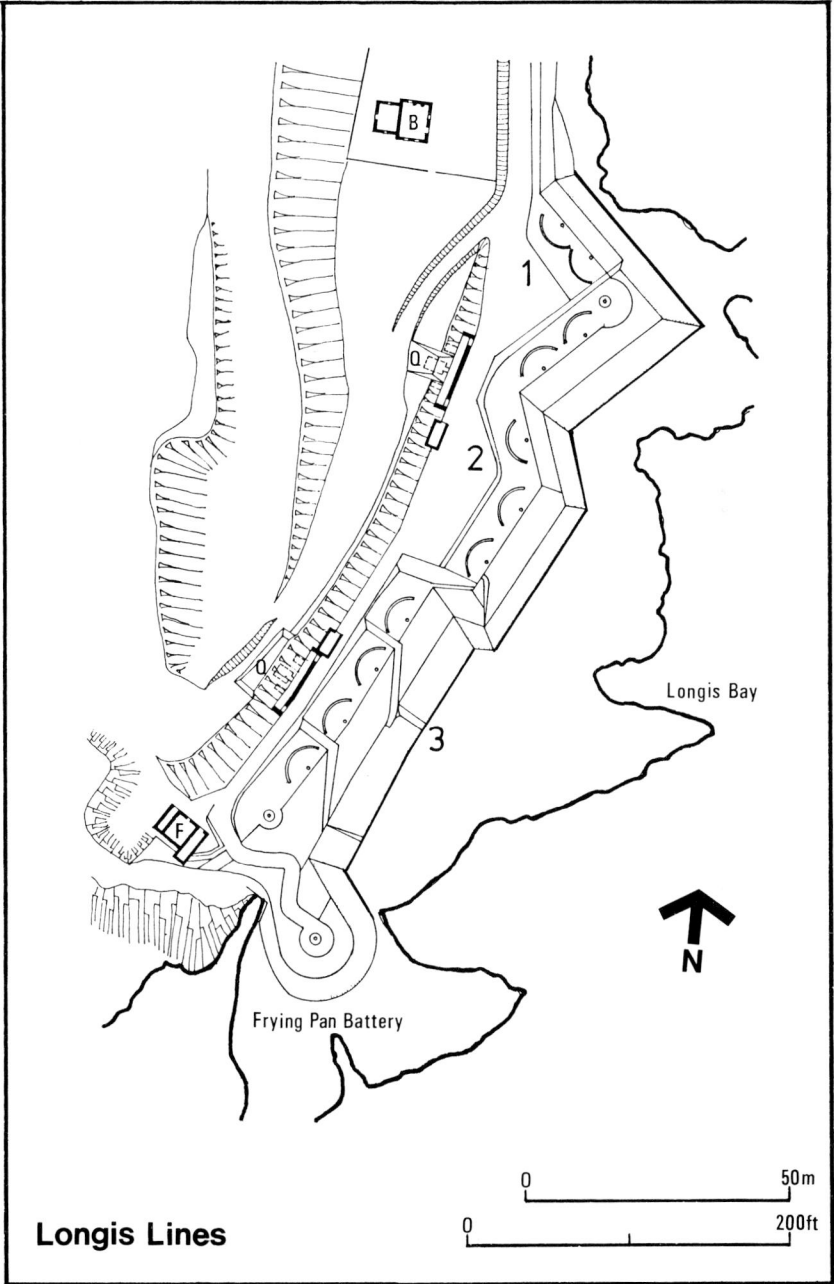

Longis Bay

N

Frying Pan Battery

0   50m

0   200ft

Longis Lines

The original entrance to Essex Barracks has two small flanking bastions with musketry loopholes.

Essex Barracks

Essex Barracks, more commonly referred to as Fort Essex, is situated on the eastern side of the crown of Essex Hill at the 196 feet (60m) level. Overlooking Longis Bay it is, perhaps, the least imposing of the works particularly with the addition of its present pitched roof. It was completed quite late in the building programme as records show that in May 1854 there were no plans in preparation for Essex Barracks; at this time it was to be designed to accommodate seven officers and 235 men. In 1869, plans were prepared and the building was converted to serve as the garrison hospital.

The north and west walls, forming part of the original sixteenth century fort, were incorporated into the Victorian work; these old walls still have the original bastions at the north-west and south-west corners. At the most northerly point of the fort, standing above the parapet, is an early nineteenth century watch tower.

The detached single storey officers' quarters are to the west of the parade, while the two storey soldiers' quarters and hospital wards are to the east overlooking the bay; small bastions flank this wall. The original entrance with guard room and flanking bastions still exists, the present entrance being unfortunately opened up after the Second World War.

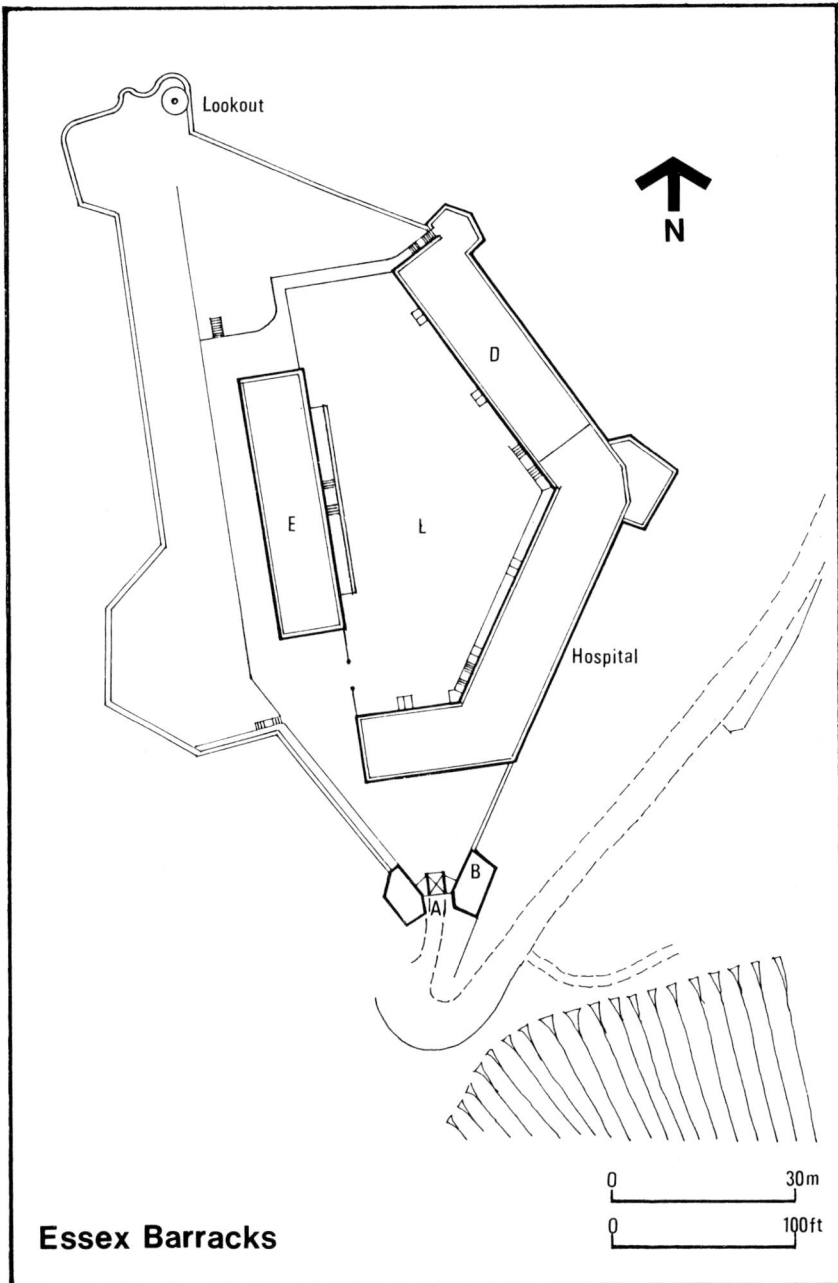

Lookout

N

D

E

L

Hospital

B

A

Essex Barracks

| 0 | 30 m |
| 0 | 100 ft |

4. THE IMPREGNABLE FORTRESS

The German Occupation

When German forces occupied the Channel Islands in the summer of 1940, no one could have foreseen that this act would lead to the final and most comprehensive programme of fortification in the history of the Islands. With each reversal in German fortunes Hitler was to retreat into a more inflexible defensive policy, and the creation of the 'Atlantic Wall' and the myth of 'Fortress Europe' were manifestations of this attitude.

For the organization and construction of such an immense programme of fortification, Hitler was able to call upon the services of the Organization Todt (OT) which had originally been set up in 1933 to construct the German motorway network. Dr Fritz Todt had been appointed Inspector-General of German Road Construction by Hitler who had recognised his engineering talents after they had come into close personal contact. However, it was not until 1938, when given control of the construction of the West Wall defences, that the Organization Todt was officially launched. After the OT had taken over construction from the Army Fortress Engineers, the work was completed within barely eighteen months. During this period, more than 14,000 installations had been constructed along 630 kilometres (400 miles) of Germany's western border.

When Hitler had decided in December 1941 that the entire continental coastline should be defended, it was the OT which assumed responsibility for the technical direction of the fortifications in co-operation with the Commander-in-Chief West. The OT was basically an organization formed from German construction companies utilising forced or impressed labourers from the occupied countries in increasing numbers after 1942. At the height of the construction programme for the Atlantic Wall in May 1943, the labour force totalled nearly half a million men of which some ten percent was German.

As a consequence of the decision to fortify the Channel Islands on a permanent basis in 1941, the OT was called in when it was realised that it was impossible for the army engineers to carry out the task alone. The main objectives were to secure the western Cotentin by artillery placed on the Islands, to protect coastal shipping and entry to the Gulf of St Malo, and the construction of airfields. During the next three years, the Islands became one of the most effectively fortified sections of the whole Atlantic Wall even though the original objectives were not reached. It has been estimated that had the resources devoted to fortifying the Islands been utilised elsewhere on the Atlantic Wall, it would have been about ten percent stronger. It

A wartime RAF aerial reconnaissance photograph of February 1945 clearly identifies the German naval coastal artillery battery Annes (Crown Copyright).

is conceivable that this could have made a considerable difference to the allied invasion in 1944. After the landings in Normandy, the Germans assumed that it would only be a matter of time before the Channel Islands were invested. However, with the inability of the Germans to secure their lines of supply, it soon became apparent that the Islands would be left isolated until the final surrender.

The Alderney garrison was to increase from 450 in 1941 to 3,200 by 1944 made up of 890 infantry, 590 navy, 1,050 air force, 70 artillery, 200 service corps and 400 auxiliary personnel. This distribution can be explained by the various command responsibilities of the German forces. The manning of anti-aircraft batteries was the responsibility of the *Lutfwaffe*, personnel being used solely in this role and not for air operations. The pre-war airfield was considered to be a potential enemy landing zone and was consequently rendered unusable. The navy was primarily responsible for coastal defence and the army batteries were subject to the direction of the local Artillery Commander who was the senior naval officer in Alderney. However, once invading troops had reached the shore, known as the main battle line, control of the landing barrage fire was assumed by the Divisional Command. Thus in Alderney, as for the whole Atlantic Wall, three types of coastal artillery battery are distinguishable, namely navy and army — both Divisional and Army Coastal Artillery — all engaging sea targets under navy control.

This view of the German Jetty at Braye was taken shortly before demolition in 1979 (K. Tough).

With the steady increase in the number of German troops and OT personnel and the arrival of enormous quantities of building materials, there was an urgent need to increase the dockside facilities. As a consequence, the structure known as the 'German jetty' was constructed in 1942. Originally designed as a heavy landing bridge for use as part of an artificial harbour for the postponed Operation 'Sealion', it was constructed of prefabricated steel sections. Sadly it had become so dilapidated that it was dismantled at great expense in 1978.

The other priority in early 1942 was for accommodation for the OT labour force. Four camps were constructed within six months by a volunteer labour force of French workmen who arrived in Alderney in January 1942. Each camp was named after a German North Sea island — Helgoland, Norderney, Borkum and Sylt — and located at Platte Saline, Saye Bay, Haize and south-west of the airfield respectively. The infamous Sylt camp, handed over to SS Construction Brigade 1 in March 1943, had been used by the OT to house Russian and other forced labourers. A full account of the treatment and conditions of the labourers in these camps is given by Pantcheff; he estimates that the average population of all four camps was between three and four thousand in 1943 and that at least 337 foreign labourers died or were killed. It is interesting to note that, at the height of the construction programme, the German garrison and OT labourers together totalled over 7,000 which exceeded the numbers involved when the British fortified the island during the Victorian period.

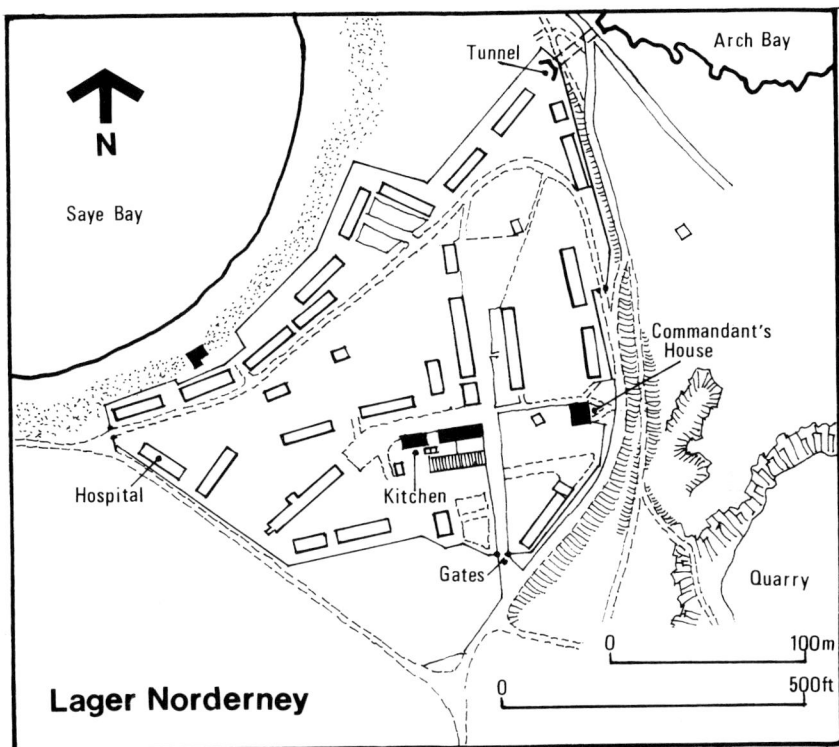

Lager Norderney

Although the majority of the permanent fortifications of the Atlantic Wall were constructed by the OT, the responsibility for their design lay with the respective units in each branch of the armed forces. In 1938 the Ministry of War was replaced by the Armed Forces High Command and, within this organisation, the Fortress Engineer section of the Army Ordnance Office pioneered the standardization of military material for Germany's West Wall, including all developments in the field of fortification design. Because of the dominant role of the Army Ordnance Office in the construction of the West Wall, the Fortress Engineer Staffs, later to be attached to the army commands along the Atlantic Wall, were able to select defence units for various sites and functions from a fully prepared schedule as were staffs from the other services. In Alderney, responsibility for the supervision of the construction of the defence works was allocated to Fortress Engineer Detachment II/11 which was subordinated to Fortress Construction Command XV in the Channel Islands.

In June 1944, the type list for the Atlantic Wall contained nearly 700 standard units which were classified as permanent defences, excluding smaller field order defences, open gun emplacements, heavy coastal batteries and other special works. For the purpose of selecting various units in the field, the Fortress Engineers of the three services were issued with a comprehensive manual containing the whole range of standard permanent defence works in reinforced concrete. These plans show recurrent features which were utilised in various combinations to suit every installation.

These features can be traced back to their immediate origin in the West Wall defences, while individual units and their layout in defensive groups can be traced back to the 'Hindenburg Line' of the First World War and the original German *Feste* constructed in the 1890s in Alsace and Lorraine. These permanent defence works were mutually supportive during an attack, the space between containing intermediate earth redoubts or batteries, and the whole area ringed with wire entanglements, trenches and machine-gun emplacements so as to form a powerful strongpoint. It was around Metz and Thionville where the *Feste* principle was developed to its greatest extent between 1900 and 1913. Perhaps the epitome of trench organisation and construction was to be seen in the 'Hindenburg Line' (or 'Siegfried Line' as it was known to the Germans); here sophisticated trench systems were backed up by reinforced concrete bunkers behind which were wide ditches to entrap tanks. From here deep passages led back to underground reinforced concrete barracks, hospitals, fire control centres and headquarters, all provided with electric light, water and telephone links.

Hitler's Directive of May 1942 established four categories of external wall and roof sections which increased with the importance of the installation. The V-weapon sites, headquarters and underground factories had wall and roof sections of 5m (16ft.4in) thick reinforced concrete (Category E), while for submarine pens, heavy gunsites and radar installations the walls were 3.5m (11ft.5in) thick (Category A). Alderney's permanent defences of standard design were generally constructed of 2m (6ft.8in) thick reinforced concrete (Category B), while improvised and field order defences of 1.2m (4ft.0in) thickness (Category B1) or less were added at a later date. The more substantial concrete works constructed to Category B specifications include casemates for 10.5cm coast defence guns and 4.7cm anti-tank guns, ammunition bunkers, anti-aircraft emplacements, observation posts, personnel shelters and command posts. Even a casual observer will soon notice certain similarities in design that are repeated in many of these works. It is this standardization of the various functional elements which permitted such a diversity of works to protect the enormous range of German and captured weapons and equipment in use in the Atlantic Wall defences.

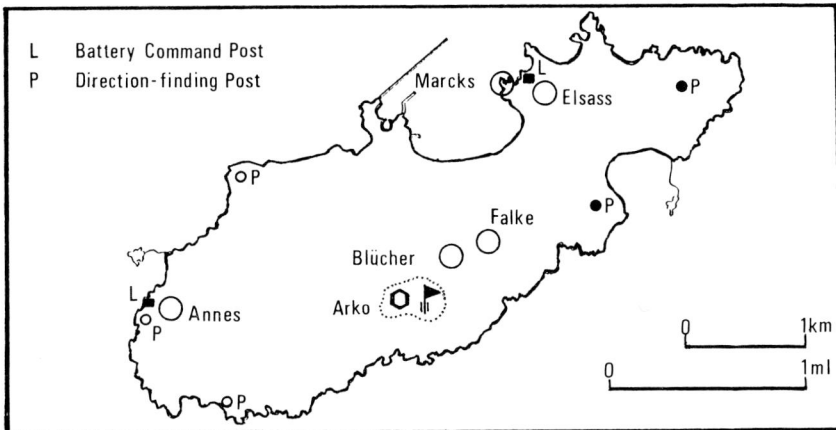

L Battery Command Post
P Direction-finding Post

Marcks

Elsass

Falke

Blücher

Arko

Annes

0   1km

0   1ml

Coastal Artillery Batteries

Guernsey, Jersey and Alderney were each treated as separate defence sectors with individual Fortress Commanders and clearly defined roles in the artillery fire plan to protect coastal traffic and entry to the Gulf of St. Malo. In this scheme Alderney was given prominence to guard the sea approaches to Cherbourg and its military role was to have a modest offensive strike capacity as well as a high defensive potential. To this end, the coordinated fire plan shows Alderney's three medium coastal artillery batteries working in conjunction with the 15.5cm and 20.3cm batteries near Cap de la Hague on the Cotentin peninsula and the 30.5cm guns of *Batterie Mirus* on Guernsey. Of the five coastal artillery batteries on Alderney, three were operated by the navy, one by the Army Coastal Artillery and one by the 319 Division.

The heaviest of these was at *Batterie Elsass* in Fort Albert mounting three 17cm SK L/40 naval guns with shields in open emplacements and having a maximum range of 22km (13 miles); the fort was also the headquarters of the naval artillery unit *Marineartillerieabteilung* (MAA) 605. In common with the two other medium batteries, machine-guns, mortars, light anti-aircraft guns, flame-throwers and searchlights were mounted within the battery perimeter for local defence. The origin of the 17cm guns of *Batterie Elsass* is of some interest. The penultimate pre-Dreadnought class of five German battleships, laid down between 1901 and 1902, was known as the *Braunschweig* class. Of the five ships, only three remained in service in the 1920s after they were converted to a coast defence role. Two were hulked in 1931 and three of the 17cm guns with their original naval shields were eventually shipped to Alderney where they were emplaced in *Batterie Elsass*. It is quite likely that the battery was named after the *Elsass*, the second of the two ships in the class.

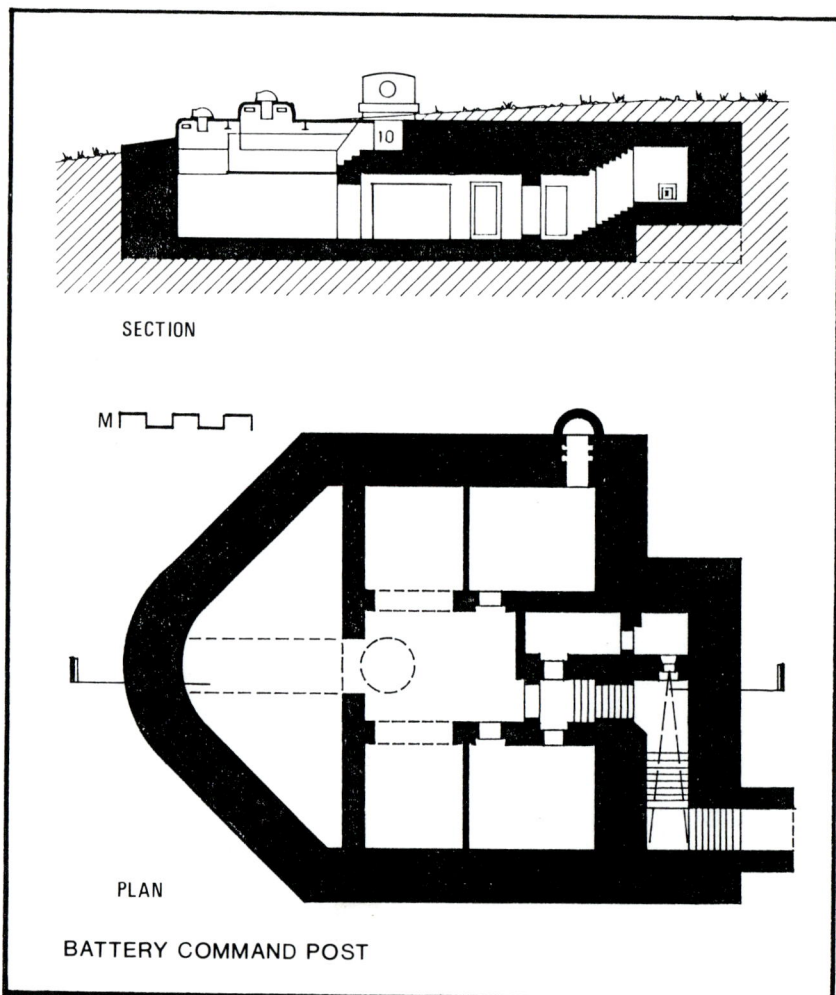

SECTION

M

PLAN

BATTERY COMMAND POST

Batterie Annes, known earlier as *Westbatterie,* was situated at the western end of the island on the Giffoine. Here four 15cm SK C/28 naval turreted guns, with an effective range of 22km (13 miles), were mounted in open concrete pits; these guns were of the same type as those of the secondary armament of the battlecruisers *Scharnhorst* and *Gneisenau.* A considerable number of other weapon positions, a barbed wire perimeter and an extensive minefield for local defence, personnel bunkers, magazines, a generator bunker and a battery command post were constructed within the battery site.

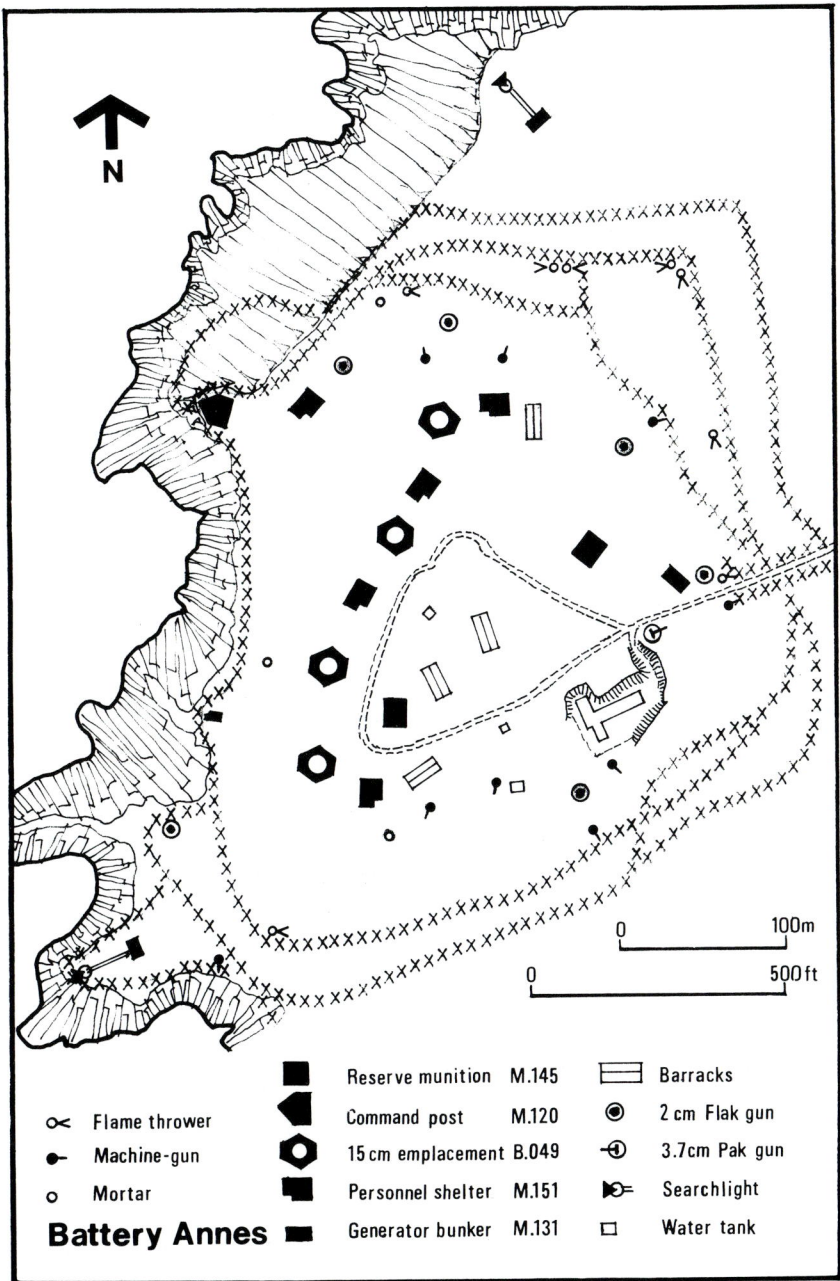

N

Battery Annes

✕	Flame thrower	■ Reserve munition M.145	⊟ Barracks
●	Machine-gun	◀ Command post M.120	◉ 2 cm Flak gun
○	Mortar	⬡ 15 cm emplacement B.049	⊕ 3.7cm Pak gun
		⬟ Personnel shelter M.151	▶= Searchlight
		▬ Generator bunker M.131	▢ Water tank

0   100m

0   500 ft

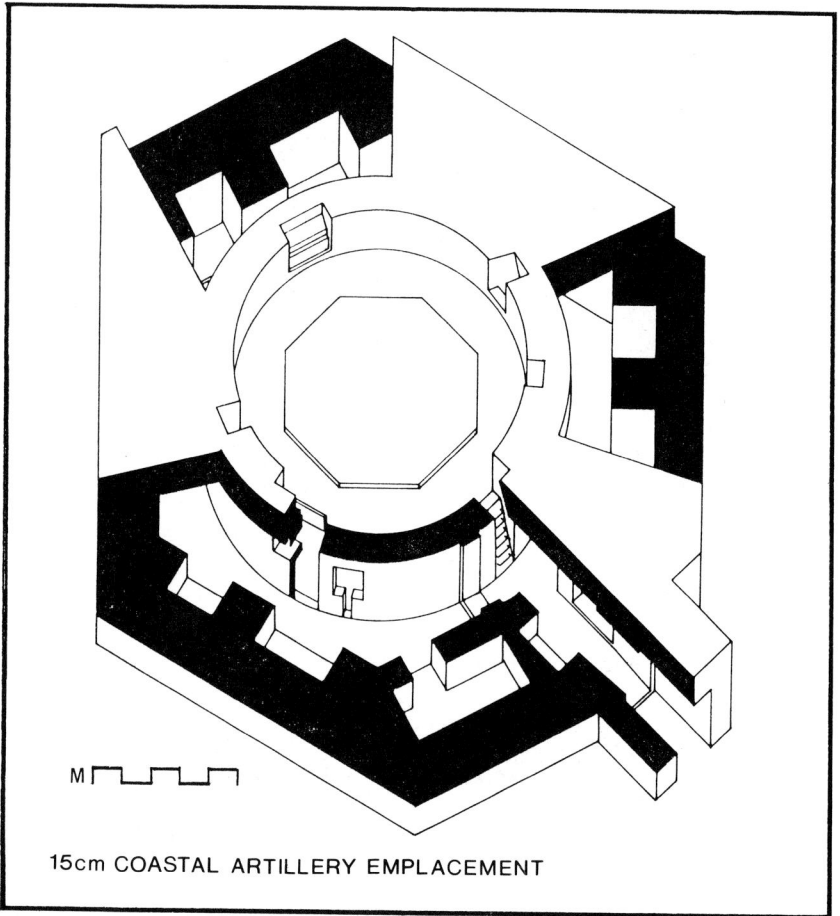

15cm COASTAL ARTILLERY EMPLACEMENT

Batteries *Annes* and *Elsass* were operated by the naval artillery unit MAA 605, while *Batterie Blücher* formed the twelfth battery of 1265 Army Coastal Artillery Battalion and was designated *Heeresküstenbatterie* (HKB) 461. Situated on the Blaye to the east of Vaindsaire, the battery mounted four 15cm K18 guns in open emplacements and, in practice, outranged the other two medium batteries by two kilometres (1.24 miles). Although originally designed as field guns, these weapons proved too cumbersome and were employed in a coastal artillery role. As with the two previous batteries, numerous smaller weapon positions were constructed for local defence, but little evidence of this battery remains apart from a crudely built small observation post at La Basse Corvée and derelict personnel shelters.

The four turreted 15 cm guns of Batterie Annes, one of which is photographed here at Liberation, were the most effective medium coastal artillery weapons in the German arsenal (RAF Museum).

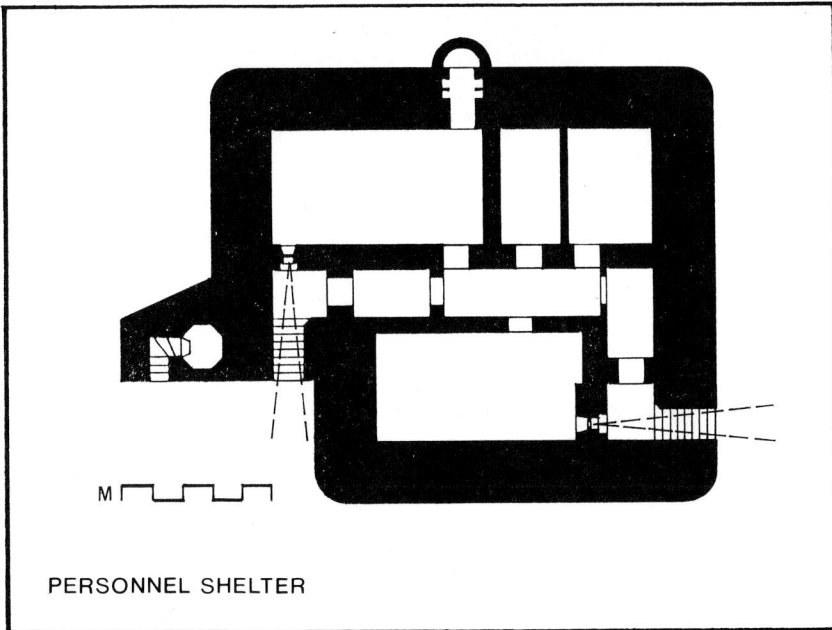

PERSONNEL SHELTER

A reconnaissance photograph taken immediately after the bombardment by HMS Rodney in August 1944 shows the pattern of shell strikes on Batterie Blücher (Public Record Office).

In June 1944, with the Americans controlling the Cotentin, the guns of *Batterie Blücher* inflicted casualties on the allied troops on the peninsula. As the density of anti-aircraft fire precluded aerial bombardment, HMS *Rodney*, which had been involved in supporting the Normandy landings, was called upon to shell the battery from a position off Cherbourg. On 12 August 1944, the battleship fired 72 rounds of 16-inch (40.6 cm) shells at the battery from a range of 40km (25 miles) using spotter aircraft to direct the fire. The result of the bombardment was two killed, several injured and the cradle and carriage of two guns damaged, while the recuperator and compensator of a third was destroyed. After being transported to Guernsey for repair, the gun was back in action in Alderney by November.

92

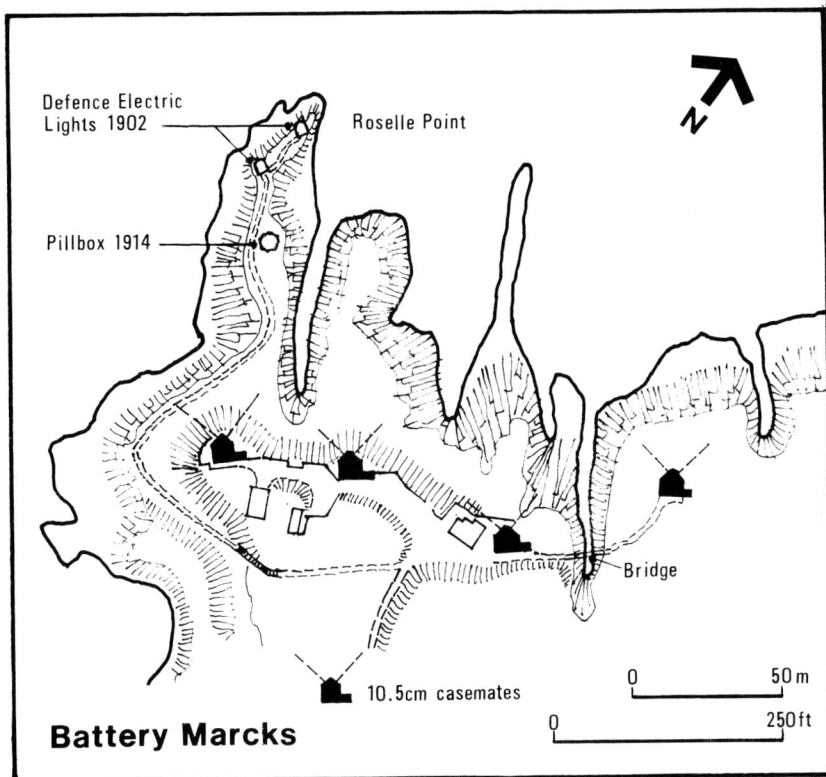

Defence Electric
Lights 1902

Roselle Point

Pillbox 1914

Bridge

10.5cm casemates

0   50 m

0   250 ft

Battery Marcks

Two other batteries of light artillery were mounted in Alderney. The casemated *Batterie Marcks*, originally known to the Germans as *Rosenbatterie*, was superimposed on the site of the old Roselle Battery. Its four French 10.5 cm K331(f) guns were manned by the naval unit MAA 605 and served to block the harbour entrance. *Batterie Falke* situated to the east of *Blücher* mounted four 10 cm leFH 14/19(t) (light Czech field howitzers) in open positions, comprising the eleventh battery of the 319 Artillery Regiment; little evidence of this battery remains on the ground. With the exception of *Marcks*, all the batteries were capable of laying down pre-determined barrage fire to any part of the shoreline in support of the beach defences.

In addition to the five principal coastal artillery batteries, a number of 10.5 cm K331(f) coast defence guns were sited at tactical positions around the island and were normally incorporated within an infantry strongpoint. The German records show a total of sixteen guns of which nine were sited in concrete casemates, the remainder being in open positions.

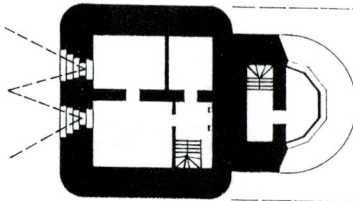

2

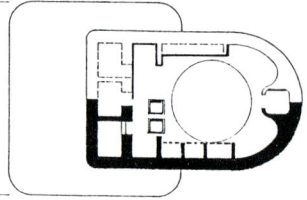

Roof

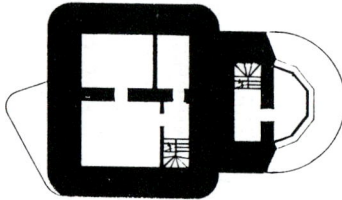

1

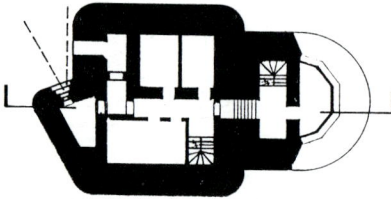

Ground

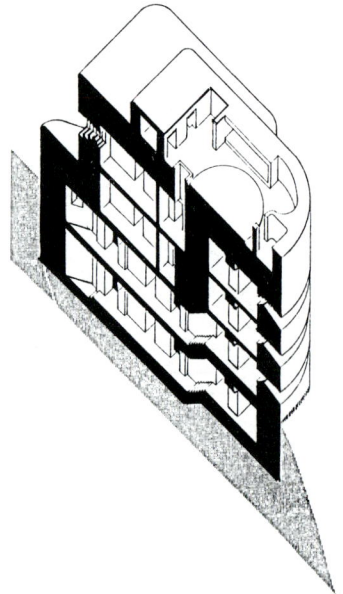

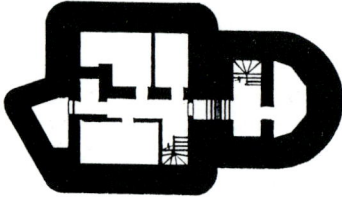

Basement

M ⌐_⌐_⌐

DIRECTION-FINDING TOWER MP3

The naval direction-finding tower at Mannez, while being a design seen nowhere else on the entire Atlantic Wall, exhibits all of the regular features of German fortification standards.

The fire of the coastal artillery batteries was coordinated from the Artillery Commander's bunker at Le Rond But, beside which stands the rusting remains of the *Freya* coast-watching radar within its crude concrete blast wall. Dominating the skyline at the eastern end of the island is the massive naval direction-finding tower, *Marinepeilstand* MP3. Each of the three floors above ground level was intended to observe the fire of a medium coastal artillery battery by working on the long base principle in concert with one of four other positions; whether these would have been of similar type is unknown. In practice, each battery, using optical range-finders, supplied information to the Artillery Commander's headquarters.

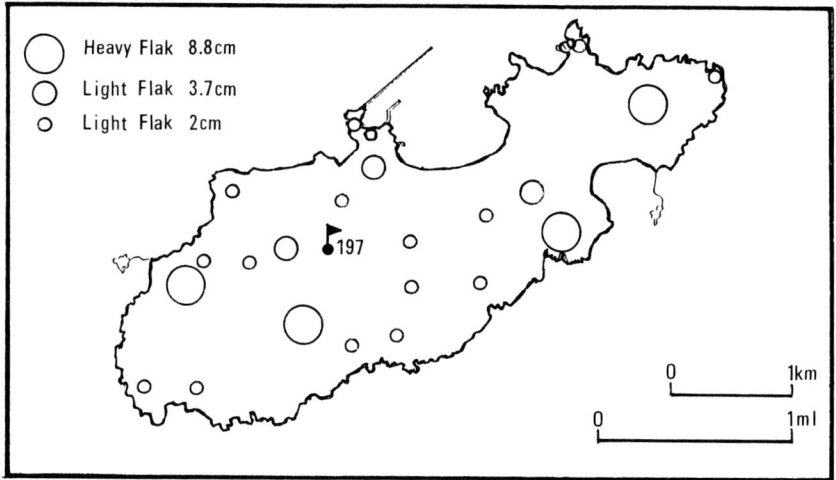

Heavy Flak 8.8cm
Light Flak 3.7cm
Light Flak 2cm

0 _____ 1km

0 _____ 1ml

Anti-Aircraft Batteries

Alderney's anti-aircraft artillery was particularly impressive for such a small island, comprising a total of 22 batteries of which four were 8.8cm installations with six guns in each. The 8.8cm batteries were located on the Giffoine above Fort Clonque, at the eastern end of the airfield, on Essex Hill and on Mannez Hill. Mannez battery is not only a fine example of a *Flak* battery built to fortress standards, but is particularly well preserved. As with the coastal artillery batteries, machine-guns, mortars and light anti-aircraft guns were mounted for local defence within the barbed wire perimeters of the major anti-aircraft sites.

Normally, 8.8cm batteries were equipped with radar and no exception was made in the case of Alderney. The *Würzburg Dora,* introduced into service at the beginning of the war, was a highly mobile anti-aircraft gun laying radar and was accurate up to 40km (25 miles). However, as these radar units needed only a flat surface from which to operate, their number and locations are not clear. The British post-war aerial photographic survey identifies what appears to be radar positions in only three of the 8.8cm sites.

It should be noted that the German 8.8cm gun performed an effective dual role; not only was it a formidable anti-aircraft gun, it was equally capable when used against tanks or other ground targets. As well as the four 8.8cm batteries, there were eighteen 2cm and 3.7cm light anti-aircraft batteries sited around the island. In addition to these batteries operated by the *Luftwaffe* which mounted a total of 87 guns, there were fourteen 2cm *Flak* guns mounted for the anti-aircraft defence of the principal coastal battery sites on the island.

96

A concrete emplacement for one of the six 8.8 cm Flak guns at Mannez with, in the distance, Fort Ile de Raz and Essex Hill.

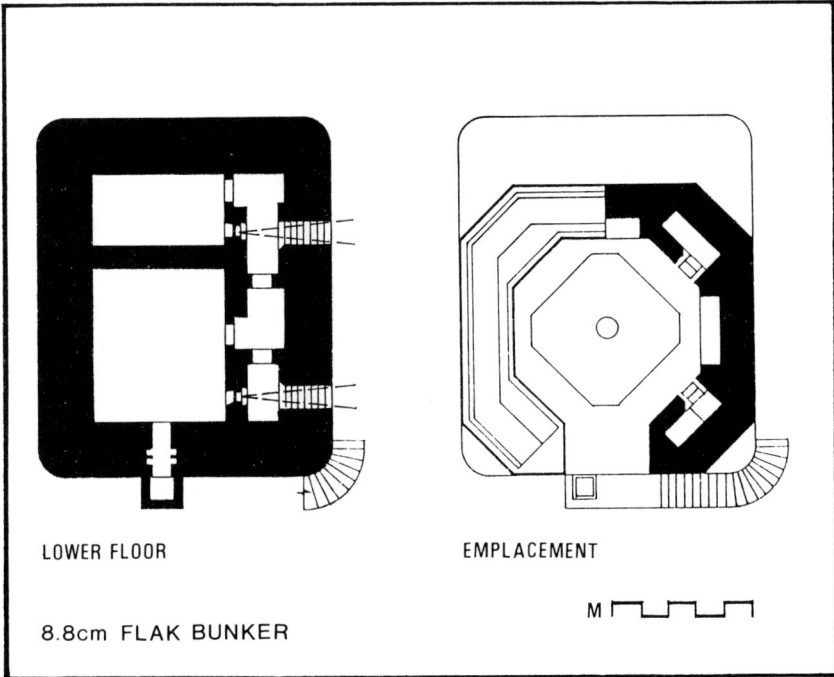

LOWER FLOOR

EMPLACEMENT

8.8cm FLAK BUNKER

M

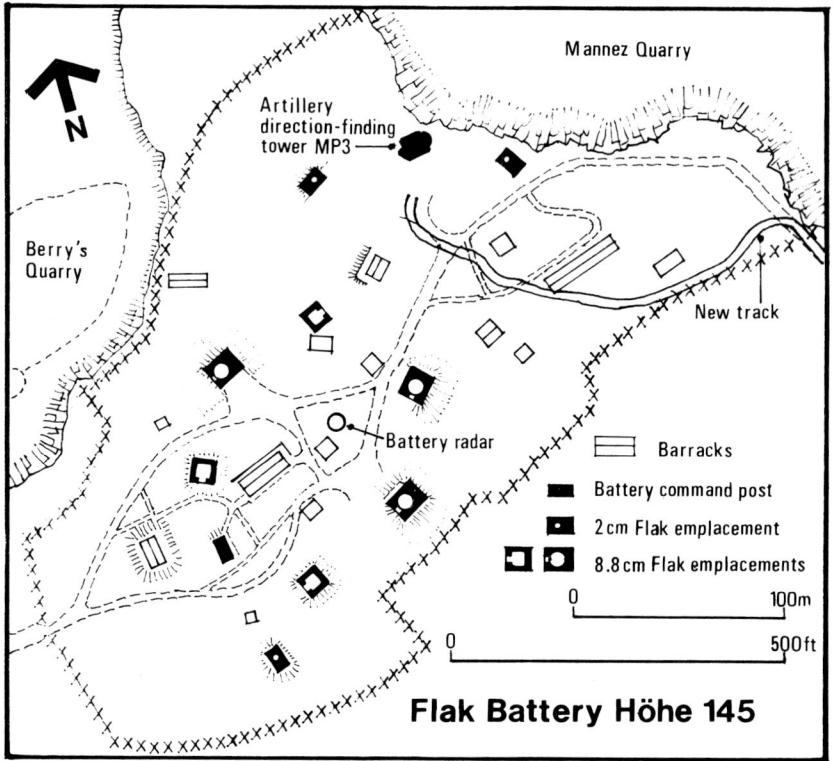

Flak Battery Höhe 145

Map legend:

Mannez Quarry

Artillery direction-finding tower MP3 →

Berry's Quarry

New track

Battery radar

Barracks

Battery command post

2 cm Flak emplacement

8.8 cm Flak emplacements

0   100m

0   500 ft

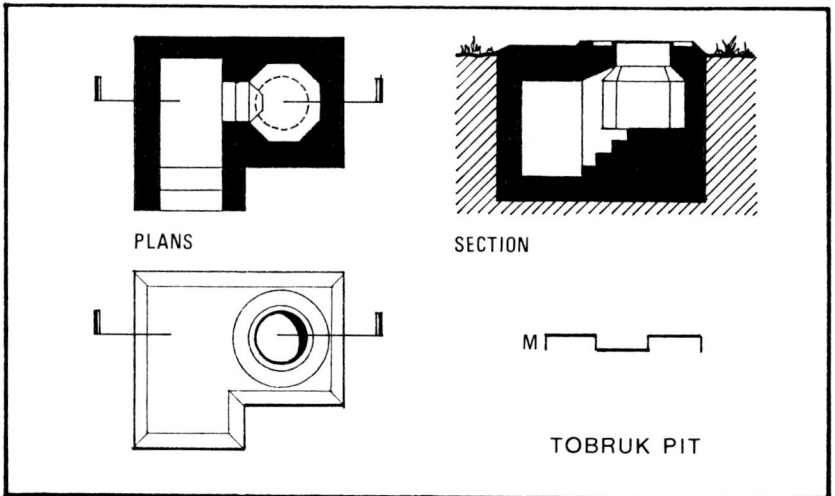

PLANS

SECTION

M

TOBRUK PIT

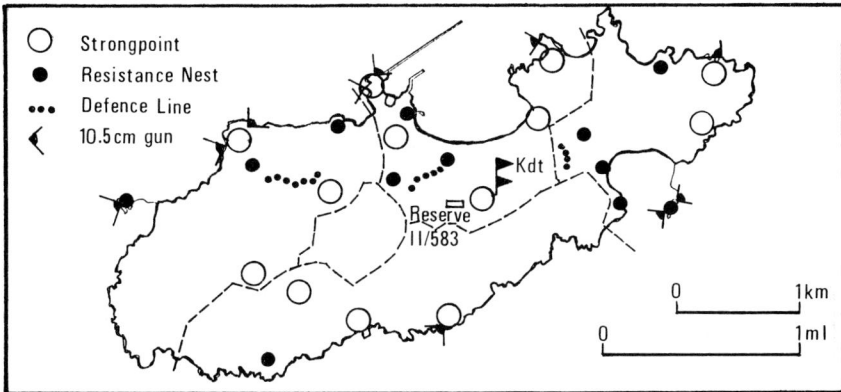

Legend:
- ○ Strongpoint
- ● Resistance Nest
- ••• Defence Line
- ◄ 10.5 cm gun

Kdt

Reserve
II/583

0 — 1 km
0 — 1 ml

Infantry Strongpoints and Resistance Nests

Guernsey and Jersey had twelve and thirteen infantry strongpoints respectively whereas Alderney, although much smaller, had thirteen also; this is a measure of the importance which the Germans attached to the defence of the island. However, the two larger islands required a greater number of infantry resistance nests and both Guernsey and Jersey had over fifty while Alderney had just twelve.

In all types of infantry strongpoints, field defences were considered essential. Machine-gun posts were sited on the flanks and in front of the permanent defence units commanding wide fields of fire. Well concealed communication trenches zig-zagged between field positions and the permanent defences. Rifle trenches and weapon pits were sited so as to cover all approaches and dead ground while small air-raid shelters were spaced at convenient intervals.

The resistance nest, sited at tactically important locations, was the smallest type of unit employed for defence against local attacks by infantry and armour. Each position was manned by one or two platoons and was self-contained, being laid out around at least one anti-tank gun with machine-gun and mortar emplacements interconnected by communication and rifle trenches. The perimeter was surrounded by barbed wire and often anti-tank and anti-personnel minefields.

The strongpoint was larger than the resistance nest. It usually comprised either a group of smaller positions having a core of heavier weapons, or a battery position for artillery or anti-aircraft support. The heavier guns were either sited in casemates or in open positions with separate units housing command posts, crew quarters and supplies. Each strongpoint was surrounded by fieldworks and manned by at least a company, while local defence was provided by light anti-aircraft guns, anti-tank guns and machine-guns.

This 10.5 cm coast defence gun casemate at Bibette Head lies within the infantry strongpoint.

The Tobruk pit originated as a small, well protected reinforced concrete position mounting a tank turret at ground level during the North African campaign. These were frequently attached to bunkers or used as independent units in field defences throughout the Atlantic Wall, and could mount a variety of different equipment from automatic weapons to the 3.7cm Renault tank turret, all of which were found in Alderney.

In Alderney, the single casemated 10.5cm coast defence guns usually formed the core of strongpoints or resistance nests. In addition, casemated anti-tank and heavy machine-guns were sited so as to enfilade the vulnerable beaches. The anti-tank guns were of three types — 4.7cm Pak(t), 5cm Pak 38 and 7.5cm Pak 40 — a total of sixteen being sited in casemates or field positions. The Czech 4.7cm anti-tank gun, brought in large numbers to the Atlantic Wall complete with co-axial machine gun and heavy armour shield, was one of the few purpose-built fortress weapons mounted in Alderney. The two types of casemate mounting these guns can be seen on Braye Beach and beside the Nunnery.

The beach at Platte Saline is defended by one of the 4.7 cm Pak(t) Czech anti-tank gun casemates.

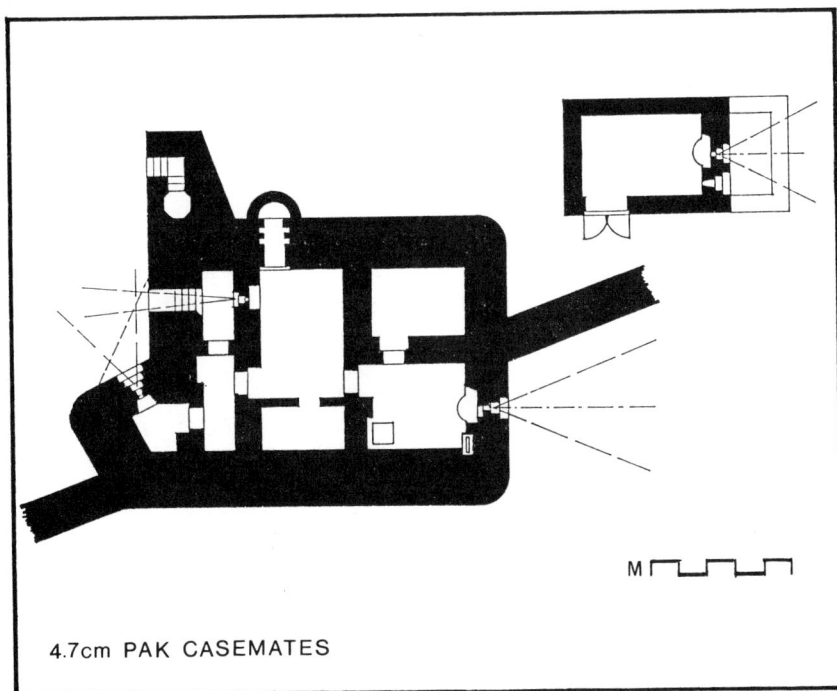

4.7cm PAK CASEMATES

M

An armoured steel cupola survives on the bunker at the northern tip of Bibette Head, with its four open machine-gun ports.

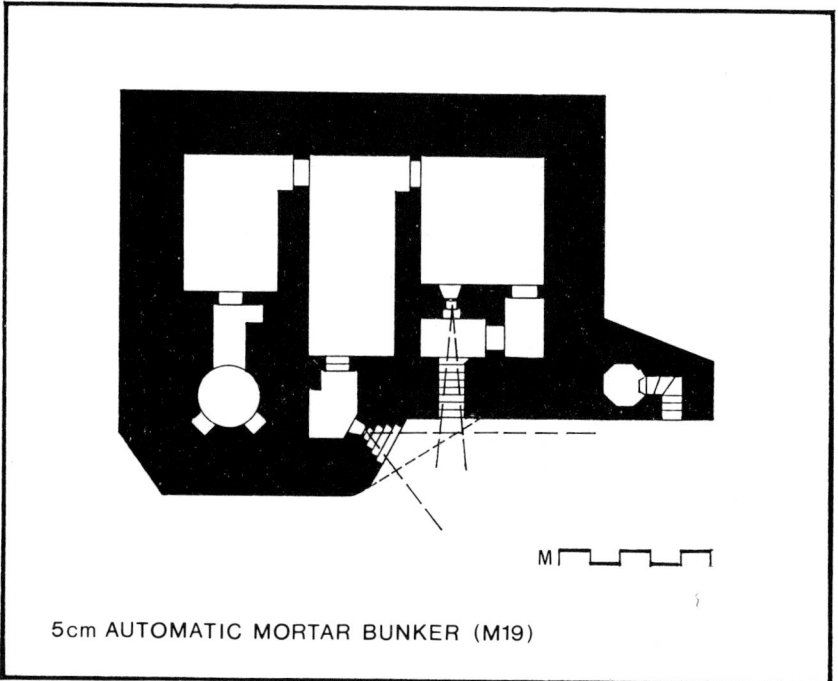

5cm AUTOMATIC MORTAR BUNKER (M19)

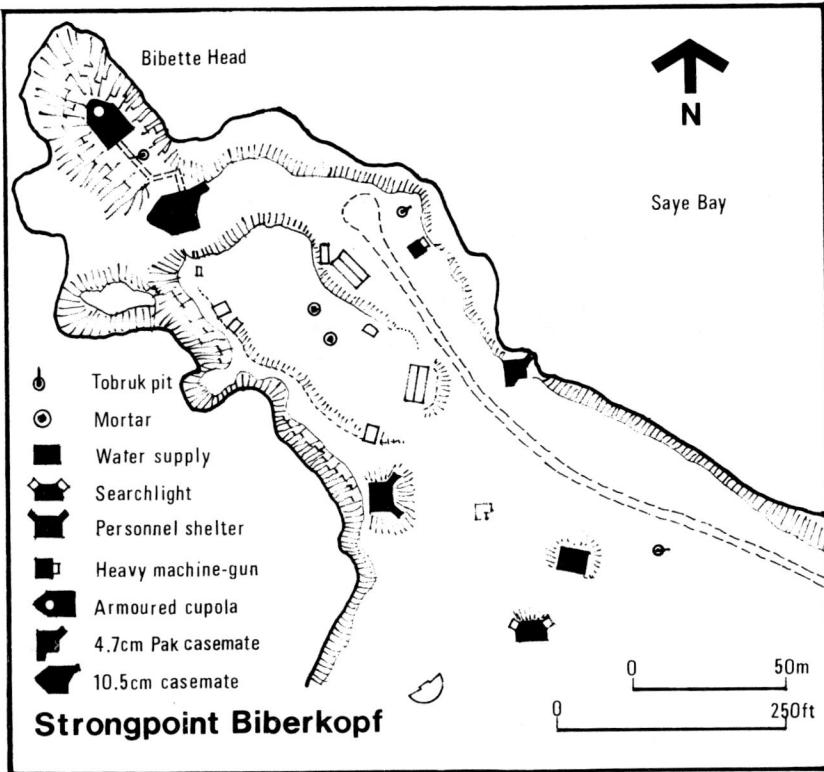

Bibette Head

N

Saye Bay

- ♦ Tobruk pit
- ◉ Mortar
- ■ Water supply
- ◈ Searchlight
- ⬙ Personnel shelter
- ⬛ Heavy machine-gun
- ◀ Armoured cupola
- ◤ 4.7cm Pak casemate
- ⬟ 10.5cm casemate

0   50m

0   250ft

Strongpoint Biberkopf

Another fortress weapon worthy of special mention was the 5cm *Maschinengranatwerfer* (M19) or automatic mortar of which Alderney boasted two. Very few of these complex weapons were installed in the Atlantic Wall defences, a number being employed in the Channel Islands. The mortar had a range of between 50 and 750 metres and was mounted in an armoured cupola and operated by a nine-man crew; bombs were fed into the mortar in six-round clips and were automatically fired at a rate of up to 120 rounds a minute. During the post-war scrap drive, the cupolas were destructively removed, but the two casemates remain to the south-east of Fort Tourgis and to the east of the track leading up Mannez Hill from the south.

Only one example of the armoured steel cupolas for heavy machine-guns remains in Alderney at the former infantry strongpoint on Bibette Head. Mounted in a fortress standard bunker at the extreme point of the headland, it commands the harbour entrance and the approaches to Braye Bay. It is linked by a tunnel to a Tobruk pit and the adjoining 10.5cm casemate.

The concrete anti-tank wall at Longis with rear firing step.

Other Defences

Further anti-tank defences were of three types — anti-tank walls, beach obstacles and mines. One of the most impressive anti-tank walls in the Channel Islands was constructed at Longis Bay, while a lower one stretches from Platte Saline Battery to Doyle's Battery. Two sorts of metal beach obstacles, tetrahedra and 'Czech hedgehogs', were erected at the gap in the Longis wall, at Douglas Quay and at Saye, Arch and Platte Saline Bays.

Out of over 30,000 mines laid in Alderney, some 1,657 were anti-tank *Teller* or plate mines. Many were laid inland as well as on the landward side of potential landing sites. A further 17,000 mines were of the standard German *Schützen* or anti-personnel pattern, while the remainder were described as 'improvised' and usually consisted of one or several artillery shells lashed together with a detonator which was activated by pressure, tension or by remote control. Large calibre shells were also used as rollbombs on the southern cliffs. The Germans effectively laid a ring of land mines and barbed wire around the whole island, as well as the major batteries.

A mobile reserve of about fifteen armoured vehicles, mostly captured obsolete Renault light tanks, was kept in three tank parks at Rose Farm, St. Martin's and near Longis House.

To prevent detection by aerial reconnaissance, camouflage was an important element in defence. The two primary methods of achieving concealment were by using earth cover with natural vegetation and the application of textured or painted surfaces, camouflage nets or dummy superstructures. Where local conditions allowed, units were set into the ground for added protection as well as concealment. The alternative was to bank earth against the structure and apply the techniques of camouflage.

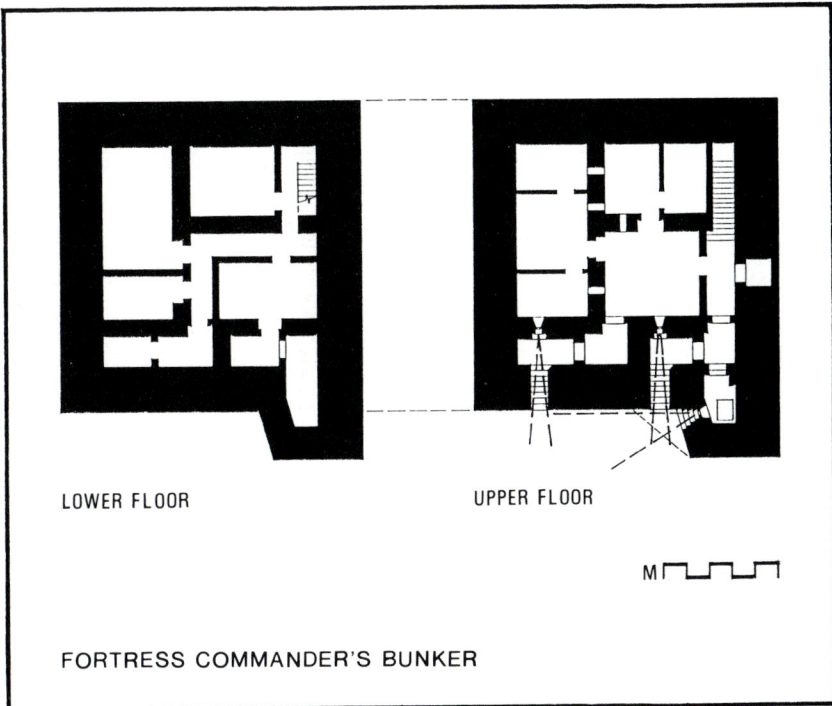

LOWER FLOOR   UPPER FLOOR

FORTRESS COMMANDER'S BUNKER

The permanent construction programme undertaken by the OT also included a substantial number of passive units, built to fortress standard, which comprised the essential infrastructure for the operational effectiveness of the active defences; most important among these was command and communications. The battle headquarters of the island commander was located in a central position at Les Rochers, and survives in excellent condition with an upper operations floor and a lower level of accommodation. It was linked by the fortress cable network to the artillery commander's bunker, the principal battery command posts and infantry strongpoints, through a series of small cable switching bunkers and a main network junction bunker sited between Whitegates and Coastguards. The distinctive tower at Les Mouriaux, which dominates the skyline of St. Anne, stands on the well-preserved *Luftwaffe* headquarters bunker and formed a link in the German coast-watching surveillance of occupied Europe. At Quatre Vents on the south coast path, the rounded, cantilevered roof of a bunker for an experimental radio signalling device, known as the *Dezimetergerät,* was built to provide an inter-island link with the continent.

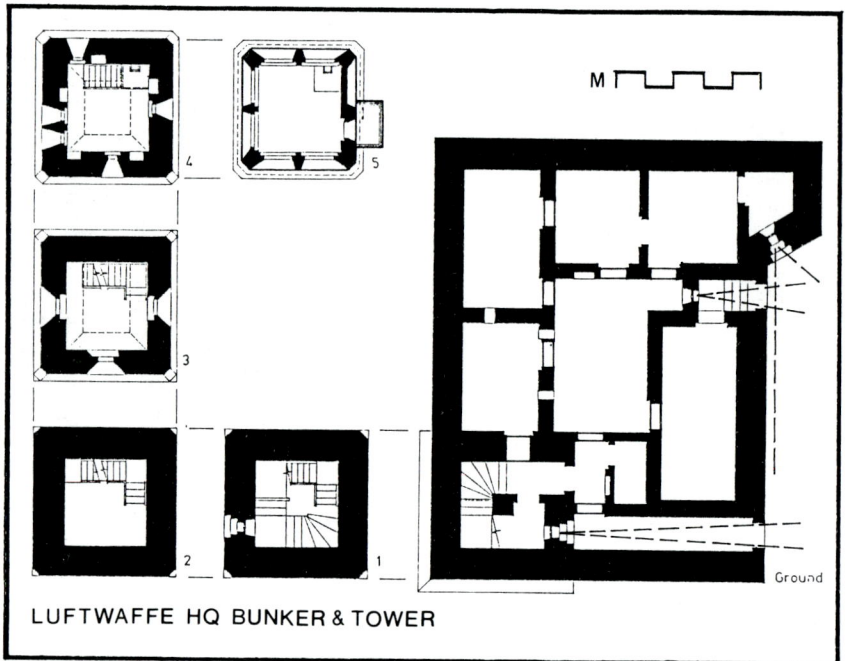

LUFTWAFFE HQ BUNKER & TOWER

Perhaps of equal importance to communications was the supply of electricity and water for the garrison. The Germans substantially increased the island's generating capacity, taking over the one pre-war facility, building three new stations and extending the supply network. In addition to these, all of the main defence concentrations had their own stand-by facilities in emergencies. There was no effective mains water supply before the occupation, and the system adopted by the Germans was to site small pumping stations on the primary sources which supplied two main storage bunkers. These bunkers were built to Category A standard and are located at the southern end of Allée ès Fées (still in use by the Water Board) and at the top of the eastern glacis of Fort Albert. A small header tank was built on the Mouriaux tower to pressurise the town supply.

In anticipation of receiving casualties under bombardment or assault, two area first aid bunkers and a central surgical unit were constructed to fortress standards. These works survive intact at Rose Farm and to the east of Whitegates, while the central hospital bunker on Longis Road is presently the headquarters of the Royal Alderney Militia cadets and the island's civil defence unit. Two large air raid shelters were built under the German extension to the eastern side of the commercial quay.

106

The impressive central hospital bunker off Longis Road remains in a well preserved state.

At an early stage in the permanent fortification programme, it was planned to excavate eight tunnels for protection and storage of reserve forces and equipment. From existing quarries or incised valleys, these tunnels were to be driven into competent rock as curving adits with openings at each end. Only four were completed at Mannez Quarry, under Essex Hill and on both sides of Water Lane (Val Reuters). Still accessible, though not to be entered without taking proper precautions, these tunnels would have provided extensive cover for mobile troops, light artillery, ammunition and fuel. Several other smaller tunnels, also still open, were driven at various other sites on the island.

The effectiveness of Alderney's German fortifications can only be a matter for debate, perhaps coloured by the performance of the defences in the Normandy invasion during early June 1944. What is certain is that the Alderney defences saw regular action, both in exercise and combat conditions, and this is recorded in detail in the war diaries of the respective armed services. The anti-aircraft defences were frequently at action stations, principally with overflights of allied air forces, and during attacks on the harbour and lighthouses which were manned by naval personnel. The coastal artillery batteries were increasingly engaged in firing on sea targets from radar and visual plots, and were stood to for regular convoy protection duty. In the most notable action — the *Rodney* bombardment — the batteries were unable to return fire due to the excessive range of the battleship. Nevertheless, the strength of the German defences in the Channel Islands had prevented any serious thoughts of assault by the allied powers.

EPILOGUE

After the withdrawal of the British garrison in 1930, the War Office retained the right of access to Fort Tourgis and Fort Albert before handing them over to the States of Alderney, and most of the smaller forts were sold to private buyers from 1934 onwards. The British Government continued to lease Fort Grosnez from the States as a depot for the maintenance of the breakwater under successive agencies until 1987 when the States of Guernsey took over responsibility for the work as part of its contribution to UK defence expenditure; it still operates the mineral railway.

At the time of going to press Essex Barracks, Chateau à L'Etoc and Rat Island Fort are privately owned and converted into flats, whilst Fort Corblets was converted to a private residence in the early 1950s. Fort Houmet Herbé, Fort Quesnard and Longis Lines are derelict, but not beyond restoration. However, Fort Les Hommeaux Florains is rapidly falling into total ruin because of its exposed position. Sadly, Fort Albert was the target for wholly unnecessary Royal Engineer exercises in 1977 when the States of Alderney permitted the demolition of the barrack blocks without supervision. The outer walls, caponiers and late Victorian magazine are under custodianship of the Alderney Fortifications Centre and although the fort is used by the cadet force and a local shooting club, it is unlikely that any restoration work will be carried out in the near future as the fort is insecure and subject to continued vandalism. Mount Hale Battery is substantially intact and the buildings which comprise the Arsenal complex are preserved, one range having been converted into flats.

Doyle's Battery was leased from the States by a local trust in 1979 and converted for use by local youth organisations, but unfortunately nearly all traces of Platte Saline Battery have become submerged in its use as a gravel works. Fort Tourgis was used after the Second World War as accommodation for Italian agricultural workers and later for visiting British service detachments. Since the late 1970s numerous redevelopment schemes have been proposed for Fort Tourgis, but no decision has yet been made as to the fort's future.

Fort Clonque has been in the ownership of the Landmark Trust since 1968 and has undergone a steady programme of restoration and conversion for use as holiday flats. It is gratifying to see the care and workmanship that has been put into the project, using the original drawings, that is surely commensurate with the exacting standards maintained by the first builders.

The many German fortifications which survive are, for the most part, in a generally well preserved state and are equally conspicuous

Fort Les Hommeaux Florains — exposed to the ravages of direct wave action and storms, is undergoing progressive collapse.

as monuments in the landscape of Alderney. Many of these lie on States land, some being available on lease; the remainder are found in private ownership.

In March 1990, the Historic Buildings & Ancient Monuments (Alderney) Law, 1989, was finally registered after a number of abortive attempts to introduce protective legislation for the island's historic architecture during the previous two decades. It is to be hoped that the principal surviving fortifications of all periods will be amongst the first works to be listed for protection. While listing in itself will not ensure their survival, it is the first and long overdue recognition by the Alderney authorities that the island's fortifications are not only of immense historic importance, but also unique and priceless assets.

APPENDIX I: Glossary

BASTION: An arrow-shaped work composed of two faces and two flanks projecting from a fort allowing flanking fire to be directed along the *escarp*.

BASTIONETTE: A small *bastion* at the corner of a barrack block.

BARBETTE: See *en barbette*.

BOX BATTERY: A box or central armoured battery mounted amidships which replaced *broadside* gun mountings on ironclad ships in the 1860s.

BROADSIDE MOUNTING: A method of mounting guns which fired through gunports along both sides of a ship's gun deck.

CAPONIER: A work defending a ditch by extending into or across it thus permitting flanking gunfire along the length of the ditch.

CARRONADE: A very short, light carriage gun using a small propellant charge to fire a relatively heavy shot for a limited range.

CITADEL: The main fortress of a town or larger fort which would both protect and dominate the major work; it also would act as a retreat for the garrison.

CAVALIER: A raised defensive battery that would act as a *traverse* and in addition would give extra height to the guns.

CASEMATE: A vaulted chamber or concrete bunker with a firing port from which artillery could be fired with overhead protection.

COUNTERFORT: A buttress built behind a *scarp wall* in order to strengthen it.

COUNTERSCARP: The exterior wall of a ditch.

EN BARBETTE: A gun firing over a parapet which has no *embrasure* is said to be mounted 'en barbette'.

ENFILADE: To sweep the whole length of any work with musketry or artillery fire.

EMBRASURE: An opening in a parapet or bunker through which a gun can be fired.

ESCARP: The inner wall of the ditch below the *rampart*.

GORGE: The rear face of a work.

GLACIS: Long gentle slope beyond the ditch stretching out towards the country.

KEEP: The stonghold or residential part of a fort.

MACHICOLATION: A projecting gallery at the top of a wall or entrance from which musketry fire can be directed downwards.

MACHICOULI: See *Machicolation*.

PARAPET: A bank or wall over which a defender may fire.

RACER: A rail, forming a horizontal arc, on which the carriage or traversing platform of a gun is moved.

RAMPART: A fortified embankment topped by a *parapet*.

REDAN: An outwork consisting of two faces forming a *salient angle*.

REDOUBT: A closed, independent work.

REVETTED DITCH: A ditch with retaining walls.

SALIENT ANGLE: Outward point of a *bastion* or other projecting work.

SALLY PORT: A small tunnel or gateway leading out of a work.

SCARP GALLERY: A chamber behind the interior wall of a ditch with loopholes for muskets.

SCARP WALL: See *escarp*.

TRACE: A ground plan of a fortification.

TRAVERSE: A barrier constructed on a parapet, etc. to protect defenders from *enfilade* or to contain the explosion of shell.

TERREPLEIN: An area behind the *parapet* of a defended work on which guns were mounted.

APPENDIX II: Fortification

Since men first assembled together for mutual protection, they have built some form of fortification for self defence. As new and more powerful means of attack were developed, the early simple defensive structures were replaced by solid stone ramparts, flanked and commanded by elevated towers. For a long period little changed until the discovery and widespread usage of gunpowder, the invention of artillery and the application of both for military purposes. This effected a revolution in the principles of attack and defence. High standing castle or city walls would no longer protect the inhabitants as artillery would soon breach the defences.

During the fifteenth century the Italians devised the 'bastion' system which, together with much lower and thicker ramparts, considerably improved the capability for defence. Bastions, arrow-shaped structures projecting from the curtain walls, replaced rounded towers and provided for a more efficient close defence. With artillery mounted on the faces firing towards the enemy, guns on the well protected flanks of the bastions could enfilade the walls and ditches during close attack.

For the next two hundred years this system was continually developed often with the addition of defensive outworks of increasing sophistication and complexity. Towards the end of the seventeeth century the art of fortification was becoming more and more a mathematical exercise. Many of these innovations were developed by the Dutch and French culminating in the systems of such eminent military engineers as Coehorn and Vauban. Vauban elaborated the bastion system employing numerous outworks on the principle of defence in depth, and for the next hundred years or so this type of fortification reigned supreme.

By the beginning of the nineteenth century, the supremacy of the various bastion systems was being questioned having been devised to protect against horizontal fire. The great development of mortars and howitzers in siege warfare during the wars of 1792–1815 resulted in enemy fire arriving vertically as well as horizontally. Engineers were also realising that too much space was taken up by guns on the flanks of the bastions in defending the walls and ditches. More importantly this reduced the direct frontal artillery defence of the fort.

Strongly influenced by the new ideas of Montalembert and Carnot, the 'polygonal' system was developed, particularly by the Germans and Austrians. The main difference between a polygonal and a bastioned fort lies in the arrangements for its defence. Instead of bastions, bomb-proof caponiers which could be powerful casemated works, were extended into or across the ditches from the lower part of the escarp; from these caponiers, the ditch could be enfiladed by small arms and/or artillery fire. Also, with the absence of bastions, the trace of the fort could be formed of straight lines resulting in a polygonal shape. All guns on the ramparts were now available for frontal fire.

Fort Albert, constructed between 1856 and 1859, was the last of the Victorian forts to be built in Alderney. Its polygonal design shows many features which set it apart from its predecessors on the island; it was designed, not only to be the strongest coastal defence work, but also to act as the main citadel should the island be overrun by an attacking force. It has a polygonal trace, deep ditches flanked by musketry caponiers and was designed to mount 43 guns.

The only other polygonal forts in the British Isles at this time were Shornmead Fort, a thirteen gun battery of the Thames defences and Forts Elson and Gomer, part of the Portsmouth defences. Shornmead was completed in 1852, but Elson and Gomer were still under construction in 1857. In 1857 Major Jervois, now Assistant to the Inspector-General of Fortifications, recommended that three new, mutually supporting forts should be built between Forts Gomer and Elson to complete the Gosport Lines and thus strengthen the western defences of Portsmouth Harbour. Begun in 1858, these three forts — Grange, Rowner and Brockhurst, together with Elson and Gomer have been described as the first 'developed polygonal' forts to be built in England. Each of the three new forts had its own self-contained, circular 'keep of last resort' complete with wet ditch; this keep would command the fort should it be overrun. These were the only polygonal forts with such keeps ever built in England as they were considered outmoded by 1860.

The original cavalier in Fort Albert, which mounted eight guns, showed many features which would have enabled it to be used as a keep of last resort. Its eastern face had a musketry parapet, while an angled parapeted lower wall at rampart level isolated the whole north-west complex of seventeen guns and the main magazine from the rest of the fort.

Jervois's posting to Alderney and his subsequent supervision of the fort construction, had a great influence on his later career, particularly in his appointment as secretary to the 1859 Royal Commision on the Defences of the United Kingdom. It was the dramatic advance in the effectiveness of the new rifled guns and the laying down of the French ironclad *Gloire* and her three sister ships in 1859 which led to the complete reorganisation of the defence of the dockyards and naval bases in Britain. This resulted in the numerous Royal Commission forts, still girdling the dockyards of Great Britain, which are sometimes referred to as 'Palmerston's Follies'. When completed these fortifications represented an advance on any in the world and for the first time since the Edwardian castles in Wales, Britain led the way in fortification design.

After 1860, the efficiency and power of artillery, warships, armour and fortification was to advance very rapidly. From this date, there was a continual battle for supremacy between the weapons and hardware of attack and defence. Forts and warships were sometimes out of date before completion, such were the advances in technology during the latter half of the nineteenth century. Alderney's fine new forts were obsolete within a few years of completion and represented one of the first casualties of this technological progress.

Key to Plans (pages 49-81)

A	Drawbridge	N	Engine Room
B	Guard Room	O	Stable
C	Magazine	P	Shell Store
D	Soldiers' Quarters	Q	Fuze-fixing Room
E	Officers' Quarters	R	Rolling Bridge
F	Artillery Store	S	Glacis
G	Kitchen	T	Cavalier
H	Caponier	U	Officers' Mess
I	Latrines	V	Staff Sergeants
J	Musketry Parapet	W	School
K	Redan	X	Sally Port
L	Parade	Y	Musketry Gallery
M	Ball Court	Z	Stores
1	Battery No. 1	3	Battery No. 3
2	Battery No. 2	4	Battery No. 4 etc.

APPENDIX III: Artillery

Since the invention of artillery, the gun had mainly been a muzzle-loading smooth-bore weapon firing spherical shot. By the 1850s, the primary heavy guns installed in British coastal defence works, including Alderney, were the 68-pounder cannon and the 8-inch shell-firing gun.

During the Crimean War, British rifled ordnance consisted of a few guns based on the unsuccessful Lancaster principle which utilised a twisted oval bore. As early as 1854 William Armstrong had proposed the need for rifled guns, as had the French, and over the next four years a series of trials began to examine and report on the merits of the different systems of rifling ordnance. A parliamentary committee recommended the Armstrong polygroove design for adoption. The Armstrong gun was a breech-loader but instead of being cast in one piece, was built up by shrinking a number of wrought iron tubes and hoops one upon another. The rifling imparted a spin to the lead-coated, elongated projectile in flight which markedly improved its stability and the range and accuracy of the gun.

Armstrong's breech-loading system was complex and there were a number of accidents due to various mechanical weaknesses. The defects of breech-loaders in Britain and other countries led to the reversion to muzzle-loading. However, the advantages of built-up construction, rifling and elongated projectiles were so numerous that the rifled muzzle-loading (RML) system was adopted both in France and Britain. The projectile now had two rows of soft copper studs which engaged on loading with three deep grooves cut in the barrel. On firing, the studs imparted spin to the projectile by riding in the grooves. To prevent the large numbers of smooth-bore guns from becoming obsolete, a Captain Palliser devised a method whereby the old barrels were bored out and a wrought-iron rifled liner was inserted. Trials showed that these converted guns were more powerful than the original smooth-bores and over 2,000 of these were made for naval and coast defence use.

The decision in 1866 to adopt the RML is often described as reactionary, but Britain along with France, Germany and Austria concluded that it was the only way to produce guns of the requisite power, particularly to overcome the new armoured ships. The zenith of these guns was reached with the 17.72-inch 100-ton guns installed with their complicated loading mechanisms in Malta and Gibraltar. Not until the early 'eighties were experts finally in agreement that the new breech-loaders were superior to the muzzle-loaders and ships and coast defences had to be re-armed.

64-pdr gun on garrison carriage.

64-pdr gun on sliding traversing carriage.

12-pdr QF (quick-firing) gun.

6-inch Mark VII BL (breech-loading) gun.

The situation at the turn of the century regarding coast defence guns was chaotic. In Britain and abroad, ports and harbours were defended by a miscellany of breech and muzzle-loaders. After studying the scale of attack to which bases and ports protected by coast defences might be subjected, it was decided to rely upon four guns, the 9.2-inch BL, 6-inch BL, 4.7-inch QF and 12-pounder QF.

Rearmament of coast defences with these weapons, at home and abroad, was started during the first five years of the new century.

APPENDIX IV: Warships

At the end of the Napoleonic Wars in 1815, the Royal Navy was unchallengeable in ships, weapons and seamen. Soon after, a rapid process of continuous technological change was to challenge every accepted concept of naval warfare. During the first half of the century the move from sail to steam, from wood to iron and from solid shot to explosive shell began a process which accelerated in the second half of the century. The introduction of rifled guns, the development of armour, the invention of mines and torpedoes and the use of steel in ship construction were to follow.

Britain, whose influence, wealth and survival depended on sea power, was faced with immense problems. It would not have been in her interest to take initiatives which would render much of her fleet obsolete. However, when change was finally accepted, Britain's lead in industrialisation allowed her to adapt quickly and easily outbuild other nations.

Despite the Anglo-French alliance in the Crimean War, France was still seen as Britain's most likely enemy. The appearance of the French wooden-hulled ironclad *Gloire* in 1859, then the most powerful ship afloat, caused some consternation. However, the British answer was swift with the launching of *Warrior* and *Black Prince;* these were iron-hulled, larger, faster and more heavily armed. The supremacy of these early ironclads did not last long. Within a few months much larger broadside ironclads, such as the 400ft (122m) *Minotaur*, were under construction.

The period from 1865 to 1880 was one of experiment which, on the whole, followed a logical course. Broadside ships gave way to central 'box battery' ships which were in turn followed by turret ships. No more British broadside ships were laid down after *Alexandra* and *Temeraire* in 1873, at which time the first true mastless ocean-going turret ship, *Devastation*, had just been completed. During this period guns were getting bigger and heavier with a corresponding increase in the thickness of armour protection. Commissioned in 1881, *Inflexible* not only had the heaviest 24-inch compound iron armour ever mounted in a battleship, but four of the largest 80-ton 16-inch muzzle-loading guns ever used by the Royal Navy.

The turret ships *Edinburgh* and *Colossus*, laid down in 1879, mark the return to heavy breech-loading rifled guns which had been abandoned by the navy after accidents with the Armstrong breech-loaders in 1862. With the laying down in 1880 of *Collingwood*, the first of the six Admiral Class barbette ships — the forerunners of the classic late-

HMS Warrior (1860).

HMS Inflexible (1880).

nineteenth century British design, experimentation was coming to an end.

By 1880, these latest designs were overshadowed by the new fear that the torpedo boat would make the battleship redundant. Neither the torpedo nor the torpedo boat were new, but by 1885, 125-ft (38m) long boats capable of over 20 knots were being built. The French were very enthusiastic as they saw these boats as a means of ending British naval predominance. Both the French and the Russians built up large fleets of these vessels which led to the introduction of numerous quick-firing and machine-guns, together with anti-torpedo nets on capital ships and finally to the torpedo boat destroyers. It should be noted that the major breakwaters of French and British ports, including Alderney's, together with harbour net barriers, search-lights and quick-firing guns, were in themselves important defence against surprise torpedo boat attack.

In 1890, British fleet manoeuvres were designed to investigate the danger of torpedo boat attack. Torpedo boats, representing 'enemy' forces, operated from Alderney with considerable success against two

117

HMS Majestic (1895).

Amiral Charnier (1897).

squadrons of ironclads and auxiliary vessels defending merchant ships in the Channel. In 1901, it was during summer manoeuvres that *Viper* — one of the fastest torpedo boat destroyers in existence — was wrecked in fog off Alderney.

As well as its torpedo boat fleet, France concentrated on building up its armoured cruiser fleet for commerce raiding in accordance with the theories of the 'jeune école'. In response, Britain laid down large numbers of 'cruisers' which included a complex variety of designs used for a variety of purposes with commerce destruction and protection being the most important.

In 1889 the important Naval Defence Act was passed and Britain introduced the 'two-Power Standard', which stated that the Royal Navy should be larger than the next two largest navies combined. This resulted in the 'Royal Sovereign' class of seven ships, the first of the pre-Dreadnoughts. Following these, a further 45 capital ships were laid down before 1906 when *Dreadnought*, the first fast all big-gun ship, rendered all previous battleships obsolete.

APPENDIX V: Tables of Armament

ARMAMENT IN 1816 — per War Office Return, 10th June 1816

	Guns		Carronades		
	24-pdr	20-pdr	18-pdr	32-pdr	Total
Longy Lines	—	5	3	2	10
Le Mesurier's Battery	—	—	3	—	3
Canard Battery	4	1	—	—	5
King's Battery	—	4	—	—	4
Stoney Hill Battery	—	—	2	—	2
Ch. à l'Etoc Battery	—	—	4	—	4
Saye Battery	2	—	—	—	2
Rozelle Battery	—	—	4	1	5
St. Anne's Battery (a)	—	7	2	—	9
Braye Battery	—	8	—	—	8
Gros Nez Battery	—	—	3	—	3
Doyle Battery	—	—	4	—	4
Platte Saline Battery	—	—	4	—	4
Rozele Battery (b)	—	—	3	—	3
Clonque Battery	2	—	2	—	4
TOTAL	8	25	34	3	70

(a) Formerly known as Elizabeth Battery, and now sited closer to the shoreline.
(b) Formerly known as Rocque Turgy Battery.

NOTES
In 1816, all batteries were recommended to be dismantled with the exception of Longy Lines, Rozelle Battery, Braye Battery and Clonque Battery, with one 20-pdr retained as a signal gun at King's Battery.

In 1826, the batteries named above which remained in commission mounted a total of 18 guns, as follows:— 2 x 24-pdr, 4 x 20-pdr, 10 x 18-pdr and 2 x 9-pdr signal guns. Braye Battery served as the saluting and practice battery.

ARMAMENT IN 1886 — per RA and RE Works Committee Report No. 33, Sept. 1886

	Mortars		Howitzers		Guns							Field Guns		Total
	13-in	8-in	10-in	8-in	8-in	7-in	68-pdr	64-pdr	40-pdr	32-pdr	24-pdr	24-pdr	9-pdr	
					RBL		RML	RBL				How		
Longis Lines	—	—	1	—	3	—	—	1	—	—	—	—	—	5
Fort Ile de Raz	—	—	—	—	—	—	—	4	—	—	—	—	—	4
Fort Houmet Herbé	—	—	—	—	—	—	3	—	—	—	—	—	—	3
Fort Quesnard	—	—	—	—	4	—	—	—	—	—	—	—	—	4
Fort Les Hommeaux Fl.	—	—	—	—	—	—	1	—	—	2	—	—	—	3
Fort Corblets	—	—	—	—	—	—	—	2	—	1	3	—	—	6
Fort Ch. à l'Étoc	—	—	—	—	4	1	4	2	—	—	—	—	—	11
Fort Albert	—	—	—	—	4	1	4	7	—	—	—	—	—	16
Roselle Battery	—	—	—	—	—	—	—	2	—	—	—	—	—	2
Braye Battery (a)	—	—	—	—	—	—	9	—	—	—	—	—	—	9
Fort Grosnez (b)	—	—	—	2	5	—	2	2	2	3	—	—	—	16
Doyle's Battery	—	—	—	—	2	—	—	—	—	—	—	—	—	2
Pl. Saline Battery (a)	—	—	—	—	—	—	5	—	—	—	—	—	—	5
Fort Tourgis (b)	—	1	—	—	6	—	4	4	—	—	2	—	—	17
Fort Clonque	—	—	—	—	1	—	1	4	—	—	—	—	—	6
Arsenal (a)	—	—	—	—	—	—	—	1	—	—	—	—	—	1
Butes Shed (a)	—	—	—	—	—	—	—	—	—	—	—	2	6	8
In Store	—	—	—	—	—	—	—	—	6	—	—	—	—	6
TOTAL	—	1	1	2	29	2(c)	33	29(d)	8(c)	6	5	2	6	124

(a) Manned by the Royal Alderney Militia.

(b) Smooth-bore guns only, manned with the help of the Royal Alderney Militia.

(c) Rifled breech-loading guns, first introduced into service in 1859, suffered many teething troubles with the breech-loading mechanism. It was not until 1885 that the services were finally prepared to acknowledge the superiority of RBL over RML guns.

(d) Probably relined 8-in and 32-pdr smooth-bore guns.

NOTES

No guns were shown at Mount Hale Battery, although a single pivot mounting exists.

By 1895, only Fort Albert and Roselle Battery remained armed, with 1 x 7-in RBL, 6 x 64-pdr RML, 4 x 8-in and 4 x 68-pdr, and 2 x 64-pdr RML respectively. The Militia then manned 2 x 9-pdr RBL field guns with 1 x 40-pdr RBL at Fort Grosnez for practice only and 5 x 40-pdr RBL in store.

At the Liberation of Alderney in May 1945, Brigadier Snow, commanding Force 135, is conducted round the coastal artillery battery on the Giffoine by a young German naval officer (RAF Museum).

ARMAMENT IN 1908 — per Alderney Defence Scheme (revised to April 1908)

	Guns				Howitzer	Machine-guns		Total
	6-in BL Mk VII	12-pdr QF	5-in BL	15-pdr BL	5-in	.303-in Maxim	.303-in Gardner	
Fort Albert	2	—	—	—	—	—	—	2
Roselle Battery	—	2	—	—	—	—	—	2
General Defence	—	—	—	6	4	8	2	20
Fort Grosnez	—	—	2	—	—	—	—	2
TOTAL	2(a)	2(a)	2(b)	6(c)	4(d)	8	2(e)	26

(a) Garrison mountings.
(b) Vavasseur mountings; used for drill and practice only.
(c) Field carriages; firing shrapnel and case shot.
(d) Field carriages; firing lyddite shell.
(e) Parapet mountings.

121

APPENDIX VI: German standardization

The design of all German fortifications in the permanent construction phase was based on well established principles of standardization, the details of which are evident in every work to be found in Alderney.

As all openings through external walls were potential weak points both in security and strength of the position, they were the subject of close study. Every unit had at least one entrance (1) and emergency exit (2), with some of the larger command posts and personnel shelters having two. The entrance, having penetrated the external wall, turns immediately through a right angle thus protecting the external bulkhead entrance door (3) from direct fire; this internal angle is always cut away at forty-five degrees on the external side to improve speed of movement. In the return wall immediately facing the entrance is a steel embrasure (4) from which a rifle or machine-gun could cover the point of entry. A second embrasure (5) at sixty degrees to the external wall was sometimes added adjacent to the entrance to provide additional flanking cover to the entrance. The main external bulkhead door was made of 4cm thick steel and was designed on the stable-door principle to allow egress should debris prevent the lower section from opening.

Emergency exits (2) were usually located in an occupied room from where a crawl duct, raised above floor level and sealed internally with a 80cm square steel door, led to a square or semi-circular vertical escape shaft (6) with step irons in the wall. Halfway along the crawl duct were two rebates one for a temporary brick wall supported on the inside by short sections of steel joists which were removable. After removing the joists, the wall could be demolished with a light charge thus allowing the occupants to crawl out. The escape shaft was concealed at the surface, but should any demolition charges be dropped into it, they would fall into the shallow well at the base and explode harmlessly.

The embrasures (7) for many of the casemated guns in the Atlantic Wall were a continual problem. In those for the West Wall, the guns had been designed specifically for fortress use with proper mountings and close tolerance armour shields. However, much of the Atlantic Wall was armed with adapted and often captured artillery firing through wide embrasures offering little protection to the gun crews. Each embrasure was designed to permit a predetermined elevation and traverse for the gun and yet afford maximum protection by carrying the roof forward on a stepped carapace (8).

It was assumed that gas warfare would be used and consequently every defence unit which had troop accommodation was designed for

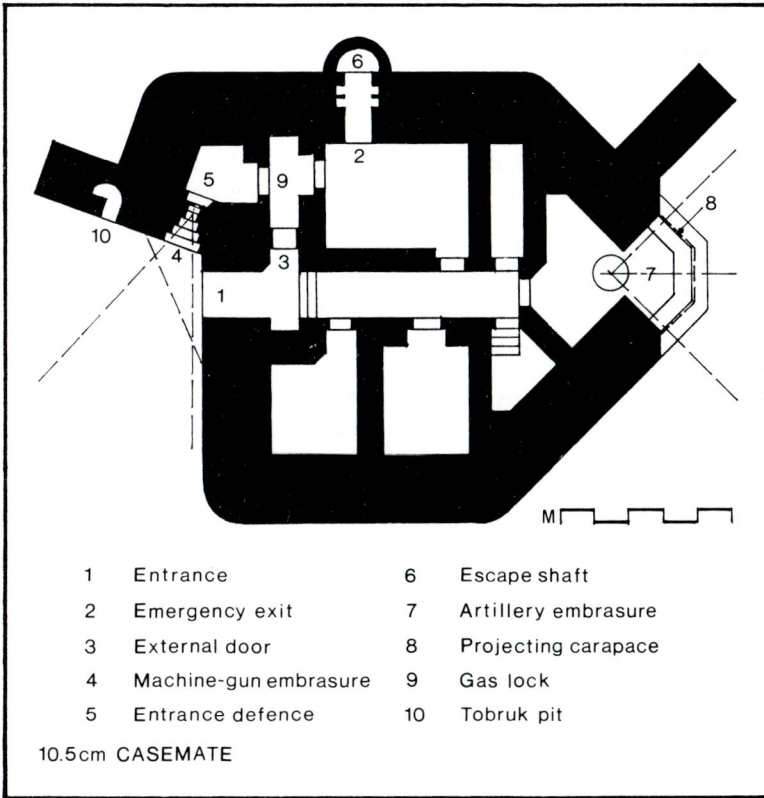

1	Entrance	6	Escape shaft
2	Emergency exit	7	Artillery embrasure
3	External door	8	Projecting carapace
4	Machine-gun embrasure	9	Gas lock
5	Entrance defence	10	Tobruk pit

10.5cm CASEMATE

protection against gas, where possible by using a gas-lock (9) at each entrance to the unit. The gas-lock prevented contaminated air from entering the occupied rooms which were provided with air drawn through filters by a mechanical or hand-operated pump at slightly higher than atmospheric pressure. Air intake for the unit was through high-level steel grilles, usually replicated, on the outside wall. Low level relief vents between rooms supplied with fresh air, permitted discharge into other internal spaces to prevent pressure build-up.

To prevent surprise attack, particularly against closed units, observation was vital. Most of the larger units had an outside observation platform known as a 'Tobruk' pit (10) communicating with the inside by means of a speaking tube. The larger personnel bunkers were often provided with a solid fuel stove with radiators and ablutions. Electricity for lighting and communications was by mains electricity or by generators in special units; smaller works had only paraffin, acetylene or carbide lamps for lighting.

BIBLIOGRAPHY

Alderney: a short history and guide, States of Alderney (1975), 3rd edition.
Alderney and the Saxon Shore, Alderney Society Bull. Vol.XVI, No.1 (1980).
All the World's Fighting Ships 1860-1905, Conway Maritime Press (1979).
G. R. Balleine: *The Tragedy of Phillippe D'Auvergne*, Phillimore (1973).
C. E. Brett: *Buildings of the Island of Alderney*, Alderney Society (1976).
C. Cruickshank: *The German Occupation of the Channel Islands*, Oxford University Press (1975).
T. G. Davenport & C. W. Partridge: *The Victorian Fortification of Alderney*, Fort, Journal: Fortress Study Group, Vol. 8 (1980).
A. H. Ewen: *Essex Castle and the Chamberlain Family*, La Soc. Guernesiaise Trans. Vol.XVI (1955-9).
Q. Hughes: *Military Architecture*, Hugh Evelyn (1974).
D. E. Johnston: *The Channel Islands: An Archaeological Guide*, Phillimore (1981).
K. W. Maurice-Jones: *The History of Coast Artillery in the British Army*, Royal Artillery Institution (1959).
M. St. J. Packe & M. Dreyfus: *The Alderney Story: 1939-1949*, Alderney Society (1971).
T. X. H. Pantcheff: *Alderney: Fortress Island*, Phillimore (1981).
C. W. Partridge: *Hitler's Atlantic Wall*, D.I. Publications (1976).
A. Saunders: *Fortress Britain*, Beaufort (1989).

SOURCES

The following archives have provided the principal sources of private and official papers, documents, plans, books, periodicals and newspapers for the content of this work.

Public Record Office, London

Admiralty correspondence, Secretary's digests, Director of Works files (ADM).
Cabinet Office memoranda, Royal correspondence (CAB).
Ministry of Defence papers (DEFE).
Home Office correspondence, papers and letterbooks (HO).
Ministry of Transport correspondence, Harbour Department (MT).
Public Record Office papers, Cabinet ministers (PRO).
Treasury correspondence (T)
War Office correspondence, Board of Ordnance papers, reports, Engineer papers, miscellaneous papers, musters/pay lists, Murray papers, maps and plans (WO).

British Library, London

House of Commons, Sessional Papers, Reports and Accounts.
Hansard's Parliamentary Debates, third and fourth series.

Journals of the House of Lords.

Additional Manuscripts: Aberdeen, Arnold-Forster, Gladstone, Goulburn, Graham, Haddington, Mackenzie, Martin, Palmerston, Peel and Wood papers.

Newspaper Library: The Times.

Royal Commission on Historical Manuscripts, London

British Cabinet Ministers: Graham, Haddington, Herbert, Murray, Palmerston, Russell, Wellington and Wood papers.

Ministry of Defence, London

Naval Historical Library: Admiralty papers, Brassey's Naval Annual, Microfilm copies captured German documents.

War Office Library: Reports, memoranda and minutes of Defence Committee meetings.

Royal Engineer Library, Chatham

Professional Papers of the Corps of Royal Engineers.

Royal Artillery Institution, Woolwich

Minutes and Proceedings of the R.A. Institution.

France

Archives de la premiere Region maritime, Cherbourg: Ports maritime de la France, Annales Maritimes, Revue Maritime et Coloniale.

Service historique de la Marine, Paris: Naval papers.

Archives du Genie, Vincennes: Engineer papers.

Germany

Bundesarchiv, Freiburg: German documents.

Bundesarchiv, Koblenz: German photographs.

United States of America

National Archives & Record Services, Washington: Microfilm of captured German documents, Class Nos. T78, T312, T314 and T1022.

Guernsey

Island Archives: maps, plans and Controlling Committee files.

Greffe Records: maps, plans and German Reference Library.

Royal Court Library: Festung Guernsey volumes.

Priaulx Library: Festung Guernsey volumes and photographs.

Guille Alles Library: Transactions, Navy & Army Illustrated and Guernsey newspapers.

German Occupation Museum: maps, plans and photographs.

Channel Islands Occupation Society: archives collection.

C.I.O.S. Occupation Review: various articles.

Alderney

Alderney Society Museum: documents, plans and photographs.

Alderney Fortifications Centre: archives collection.

INDEX

The names of forts and batteries are cited with names and locations first.